SKILLS
FOR
SUCCESS

THE
EXPERTS
SHOW THE WAY

Edited by the Soundview Editorial Staff

TABLE OF CONTENTS

INTRODUCTION

Is there a secret of success? Does one concept or strategy enable you, if you master it, to develop and improve the skills, abilities, and even character traits that lead to success?

The answer is a qualified "no."

However, many books explain proven approaches that can boost your chances for success. Some present a broad strategy for developing the traits and life skills you need to make it in today's competitive world. Others zero in on specific areas such as communicating, decision-making, and time management.

For more than ten years, Soundview Executive Book Summaries has published condensed versions of thought-provoking and useful current and classic business books. The Soundview format presents the meat of each book in newsletter-length summaries. Subscribers read the key points and important details of each book. Thus, even the busiest people can benefit from the information, ideas, and suggestions that are shaping business thinking and building successful careers today.

Soundview has selected ideas from some of the best summaries of recent years to create this book. A guide to specific strategies and techniques, it is written to help you at any stage in life to make the most of your skills and abilities, to speed your career development and improve your working relationships. You'll find ideas you can use today on everything from enhancing your own creativity to reducing paperwork to motivating other people.

Like the Soundview Summaries, the book keeps the focus on specifics. The more than thirty Summaries used in this book were selected because they provide concrete strategies and techniques you can use now.

The book is divided into three parts. They present ways to make the most of yourself, your career, and your working relationships. These three subject areas are, of course, interrelated, and most of the skills and abilities covered are as valuable for personal success and satisfaction as they are for getting ahead in your career.

Not every approach will work for everyone. That's why you'll find several ways, for example, to strengthen the process you use to make decisions.

No matter what your age, job, career stage, or goals, you'll discover ways to make the most of your potential, to be what you want to be and can be. The executives and consultants who wrote the books included here are, like you, operating in the complex and competitive real world. Their practical strategies and ideas take into account the problems and pitfalls we all encounter, and offer ways to deal with them.

There is no one secret of success, but there are hundreds of not-so-secret ways to achieve it. You'll find them in this book and in the Soundview Executive Book Summaries from which they are taken. And you will learn about them quickly. The book recognizes that your time is valuable and that you want to make the most of that time to make the most of your life.

PART I

HOW TO GET THE MOST FROM YOURSELF

W hen we look for ways to improve, we all tend to focus on specific narrow areas, on traits we don't like about ourselves or on measurable skills we would like to acquire or improve.

We take for granted many of our vital skills and abilities, not realizing they can be developed and improved. These skills and abilities can make you more effective and efficient, on the job and off. They're critical to success, and mastering them will give you greater satisfaction and the confidence you need to forge ahead.

This first part of the book looks first at the concept of success. It offers several thought-provoking perspectives on what it means and what it takes to succeed.

The next topic, Set Goals for Yourself, helps you to focus on where you want to go and what you want to be. Setting goals means you're not drifting with the winds in your career. It means you're establishing long-term goals for your career and short-term goals for what you will accomplish today and this week to move you in the direction of those long-term goals. It means your every move is made with those goals foremost in your mind.

Read the life stories of famous men and women. All of them set goals for themselves, then never deviated from the paths that led to those goals.

Part I looks at five key life skills: creativity, listening, speaking, reading, and decision-making. Many people view the way they handle, or don't handle, these day-to-day aspects of life as unchangeable. But they are learned approaches, and you'll find a variety of techniques to help you to develop, refine, and master them.

Finally, you'll learn how to manage stress, an unavoidable part of life. Stress is often regarded as simply an unpleasant fact. But it can be reduced and directed to minimize its negative aspects and maximize its positive ones.

Closely allied to stress is the number one fear of many in business today — burnout. We will take a quick look at that, to understand what burnout is, and how you and your organization often can turn it from something to be feared to something that helps to move your career forward.

Chapter 1

You Can Be Successful

We all want to be proud of who we are and what we've accomplished. We want the satisfaction of knowing we're making the most of our potential. In short, we all want to be successful in our own eyes and in the eyes of others.

But what exactly is success? What makes a person successful, someone others look up to and turn to for direction?

Even more important, how do you join the ranks? How do you grow and advance and reach a point in life that you would be happy to define as successful?

There is, according to George Gallup Jr. and Alec M. Gallup, a "success personality." In *The Great American Success Story,* a book based on a survey of 1500 successful people, they list characteristics typical of those who reach the top of the ladder:

1. Common Sense. Successful people can make sound judgments on the everyday affairs of life and brush away extraneous, irrelevant thoughts and ideas to get to the core of what matters.

The humorist Dr. Charles Jarvis said we all have a lot of it because we certainly "ain't used any." That's not so with the achievers. In their survey, the Gallups found a strong majority listing common sense as the cornerstone of their successes. A Texas oil magnate looked on common sense, in part, as the ability "to reduce one's understanding of a complex problem to the simplest terms."

2. Specialized knowledge of your field. This results from making an effort to keep learning constantly throughout life.

"Do your homework," said an industrial corporate leader. "Nothing helps success more than knowing what you're doing. It reduces the risks and works like an insurance policy for your own stability."

Another corporate official seconded this, then said that in order to achieve success, you must want it. He paused, then added, "Then you must work to keep it."

3. Self-reliance. This is the courage to get things moving in life, relying primarily on your own resources and abilities. You do so by setting goals and exerting plain old willpower.

4. General intelligence. The achievers polled indicated they meant something specific when they mentioned intelligence. They looked on it as a high IQ, an extensive vocabulary, good reading skills, and good writing skills.

5. The ability to get things done. Successful people are diligent and hard-working. They have good organizational abilities and productive work habits and can distinguish between what is important and what is not. That doesn't mean being a compulsive perfectionist who strives endlessly toward impossible goals, terrified by the threat of failure and never feeling rewarded by accomplishments.

6. Leadership. Successful people lead through motivation, not intimidation.

7. Knowing right from wrong. It's important to be sensitive to moral and ethical concerns.

8. Creativity. Natural talent plus insight or intuition equal creativity. Natural gifts are not, however, as important as making the best use of your abilities. Even an artist rated his hard work over his talent as the reason for his broad public acceptance. That same artist put ambition, motivation, and a desire to excel before his talent.

9. Self-confidence. This feeling of assurance is based on knowing you've done everything possible to prepare. It doesn't imply a willingness to take foolhardy risks, but it does indicate a willingness to strike out in new, uncharted directions.

10. Oral expression. This is the ability to get your message across, even in front of a large group.

The noted investor John Templeton figured out an approach to public speaking when he was in high school. He stood before an audience of more than 100 persons — "and . . . I understood the meaning of stage fright."

It didn't stop him. He reasoned with himself that he wasn't perfect, but nobody expected him to be perfect. "All I can do is the best job I know how. If I pray ahead of time, I'm likely to do as well as God wants me to. So there's no reason to be shy or frightened about it."

11. Concern for others. At the very least, successful people can get along with others.

12. Luck. Luck always helps, but it's never enough. The head of a major insurance firm expressed his thoughts about luck this way: "Given basic education and good health, it seems to me that individual drive, initiative, and efficient hard work are the ingredients of success — provided the person has a well-balanced personality and high ethical standards. These attributes will position you to exploit good luck and contain the effects of bad luck."

The true achievers interviewed agreed on something most of those striving for success might not believe:

The monetary measures of success — a lot of money, extra homes and cars, and other trappings — lose their importance, once achieved. But the achievers continue to strive for a sense of personal worth and self-respect. And they value — and many of them still desperately seek — those two elusive benefits, great happiness and satisfaction.

Check Yourself

Stephen Strasser, author of *Working It Out,* believes that persons intent on success should first check and improve characteristics linked with their interpersonal relationships. Here are four of them:

1. Empathy. Empathetic managers and employees express to others a sense of understanding and compassion.

One manager showed this in a simple way. Employees often expressed to him a multitude of work frustrations, career disappointments, and even their personal family problems. All got the impression that the boss really understood how they felt. His secret was that he would listen — intently. He said virtually nothing, but his attitude said a lot. He showed compassion and understanding, but never pity. And he made them move toward a solution. "What are you going to do about it?" he would ask. "And what can I do to help you get exactly what you want?"

2. Humor. Being able to laugh at yourself is one of the greatest talents that skilled persons have. It tells others you will take responsibility for your mistakes. Revealing some of your human frailties, opening yourself up, sharing your personal self, all those contribute to solid interpersonal relationships. But keep humor positive. There is nothing less funny than hurtful sarcasm or putdowns.

3. Courtesy. Common courtesy helps to build strong relationships. It also creates long-lasting impressions of you. By being courteous, you are telling others you are thinking of someone other than yourself, you are treating others as you wish to be treated, and you are an approachable person, willing to engage in a relationship.

4. Building trust. To get the trust of others, you must demonstrate that you will never breach their confidence, that you will be honest, and that you have their self-interest in mind. Words to others usually aren't enough. Only actions — your actions — count.

Winners and Losers

George Sullivan explores definitions of success in his book *Work Smart, Not Hard,* which divides people into winners and losers. Winners, he says, have critical skills that they've developed to a high degree. They don't leave winning to chance; they make it happen. Winners usually have these qualities:

● **The success mindset.** They have a winning attitude. They're enthusiastic about their work. Under stress, they have no doubt about themselves. There's pride and self-esteem involved. They have both a desire for and an expectation of success. Persons who fail often have the desire but not the expectation.

• **Setting goals.** Winners are single-minded in setting, then pursuing goals. Your main goals should be five or ten years in the future, and should involve more than a good salary or lavish perks. Without goals, chance and circumstance will determine where you'll go. You also need short-range goals, for today, next week, and next month. Achieving those enables you to attain your long-range goals. Having goals increases your efficiency and effectiveness, and makes it easier for you to make decisions.

• **The education advantage.** Education pays big dividends in terms of winning. While many of the dividends of an education aren't measurable, some, such as salaries, are, and they demonstrate conclusively that money spent on education is well spent.

• **Controlling others.** Winners need to deal effectively with other people. Some do it intuitively, others learn it. They know what makes people tick. They really care about others. They're good listeners and quick to show appreciation. They avoid head-on collisions with people, realizing a heated argument accomplishes nothing.

• **Playing the part.** This means dressing in a way that says success. It means being able to present ideas clearly and with authority, and doing this in front of a group as well as on paper.

Achievers

In *The Achievers,* Raymond Johnson takes a different look at success. Achievers, he says, are workers. They enjoy what they do.

If you want to be an achiever, Johnson suggests, clearly define what you mean by work. The average person knows what it means to his bank account. The achiever knows what it means to his life.

Find a Mentor

If you can get competent help to advance your career, use it, advises Jeffrey P. Davidson, author of *Blow Your Own Horn.*

This help often can be a mentor, a senior executive who is ready to guide you through the learning process and introduce you to associates.

There can be disadvantages to this relationship. Mentors must spend a lot of time away from other work, a failure by one can embarrass the other, and emotional dependency can grow on either side.

The Best Mentor

The best possible mentor is an executive who has retired and who can assist with chronicling the events leading up to current political situations, even though that person now is out of the mainstream of company politics.

Seek as much help and advice as you can from as many sources as possible. Don't necessarily isolate your efforts to finding just one mentor.

Career Counselor

Another possibility is to use a good career counselor. Only a few hours of assistance each month may keep you on track. Don't hesitate to use this help. Think of it the way Olympic athletes do. As they rise in the ranks, they find that each move becomes more and more critical, and they have learned that the coach can give them the competitive edge.

Some achievers see using "professional help" as a weakness. Far from it. You are still doing everything on your own. The career counselor only helps you to do it better.

If you decide to seek help, talk with possible counselors, asking about their training, experience, specialties, and fee and payment arrangements. If a person is not quite right for you, go to another.

Chapter 2

Set Goals for Yourself

Successful people succeed because they know where they want to go.

You must decide what you want to be and what you want to accomplish. The best way is to set goals that will point you in the right direction. Goals will also help you to determine when you've arrived — or if you have gotten off the track.

Areas to Cover

Goals must be specific, and they must cover many areas. It's not enough simply to decide you want to have a million dollars or be president of your company. In *Work Smart, Not Hard,* Sullivan suggests that you set goals in these categories:

- **Career.** Reach a certain professional level, get promoted, be given greater responsibility, learn a new job skill, complete a project in a specific amount of time.
- **Financial.** Earn a certain amount of money in a specified time, get a raise, set up an investment program.
- **Educational.** Earn credits toward a degree, take courses in subjects in which you've always been interested.
- **Physical fitness.** Jog three or four times a week, quit smoking, join a health club, diet.
- **Community/charity.** Do volunteer work at the hospital, sign up with Literacy Volunteers or a similar organization.
- **Personal.** Work to become less anxious, hostile, jealous, or insecure; meet new people, cultivate new friendships.
- **Leisure.** Do something different — go whale-watching, visit a country or city you've never been to before, join an archaeological dig in Mexico.

Planning Your Goals

As you plan your personal life goals, ask yourself what else you want in life, what changes you hope to make in yourself and your environment, advises Charles R. Hobbs, author of *Time Power.* Dream a little. You have your whole life to accomplish these goals, so think of your major interests and assess your abilities realistically.

Few people undertake this type of analysis, often because they're reluctant to leave their "comfort zones," the areas such as the office and the home where they feel most at ease. To set and achieve goals, you have to move out of those zones and stretch yourself.

The areas for personal life goals recommended by Hobbs are different than those suggested by Sullivan. Hobbs urges you to plan at least one personal life goal in each of the six categories that add up to a balanced life: spiritual, professional, financial, social, intellectual and cultural, and physical and recreational.

Write Them Down

Write each of your goals at the top of a sheet of paper. Now think of the ways to reach them, and write them down. These will be your intermediate goals, and they should be prioritized.

As an example, if your long-range financial goal is to have a net worth of $1 million by the time you retire, an intermediate goal might be to start by investing $2,000 this year in a growth mutual fund.

A long-range goal of maintaining excellent health might include an intermediate goal of having an annual physical examination. Make such a goal specific. Have a physical every December. Then, when you are listing your immediate goals, you will write, "Make an appointment for an annual physical on December 1."

Make Goals Specific

It's important to keep goals specific and measurable. One good way is to date them, such as "By August 1, I will . . ."

For goals where dates don't apply, such as "I will exercise daily," assign a beginning date.

Putting goals in writing is important, but that doesn't mean carving them in stone. Be adaptable if circumstances call for change.

Make your goals a part of your daily life. Commit at least thirty minutes first thing every morning to a planning session when you will translate your long-range and intermediate goals into immediate goals. These will be the prioritized items that will make up your daily action list.

Setting Priorities

Sullivan notes that it takes many steps to reach your goals, so deciding which steps to take means you must set priorities about your daily activities, so they fit with the goals.

Tom Landry of the Dallas Cowboys uses a method told to him years ago. At the end of each day, he lists on paper all the things he must do the next day. Then he numbers them in the order of importance. He carries this list, and checks each item off as he accomplishes it. He doesn't worry at the end of the day whether he hasn't completed all of them, because he has worked on the most important ones.

Says Landry, "I have used this same idea for many years and have found that I can accomplish more things with this method than with any other idea I have ever received."

A refinement of this is to use the list to make a daily schedule, blocking out chunks of time to handle the most important items.

Enjoy Reaching Goals

Stephen Strasser, in *Working It Out,* offers some guidelines to make your selection of goals a greater success. He promises that if you follow these rules, you'll learn that the process of attaining goals is fully as satisfying as actually reaching them.

Goals, says Strasser, must be concrete, measurable, and understandable. "I want to be rich" is a goal that breaks that rule. It's understandable — but that's all.

They must be attainable. Goals that are impossible shouldn't be called goals. They're simply daydreams.

They must be challenging. If you set goals that are too easy to attain, you'll lose interest in them.

You need feedback on whether you are attaining them. Short-term goals help in such cases. It may be difficult to judge whether you are making progress on a goal to "Get an education." You get immediate feedback at the end of a term if your goal is to get a specific number of credits toward a college diploma.

Finally, you must value your goals and find their pursuit personally meaningful.

By following these suggestions when you draw up your goals, you'll find you are focusing your attention and energies, and you will be moved to make action plans to attain them.

Three authors, Matthew J. Culligan, Suzanne Deakins, and Arthur Young, in their book, *Back-to-Basics Management,* provide some concrete suggestions for goal-setting. They define goals as the internalized drives that make all of us go.

Look At Yourself

They say the first step in setting goals is to take a long look at yourself. Form a picture in your mind as to what you want that reflection to look like.

Write down your financial and personal goals in time sequences. Make a list of what must be done to achieve them. Then break it down even further by goals for career, physical, family, attitude, education, and entertainment.

And, when you've finished them, don't set them aside. You must work on your goals every day. That doesn't mean working on every goal every day;

it does mean working every day, keeping your whole system pointed in the direction of action.

Special Handling

You've probably selected goals in categories where you've been less than successful in the past. If so, give these special handling. Visualize yourself completing them — every day. When you speak of them, say "I have decided to . . ." rather than "I have to . . ." Talk about them and yourself in positive terms, focusing on the rewards of success, not the cost of failure. When you have written down these goals, show them to someone who can help you to accomplish them. Act and think like a winner.

The authors of *Back-to-Basics Management* conclude with this thought: The key to being organized is not penciling notes on your calender, but rather applying self-discipline to your system. It takes more than writing out a set of goals to make them influence your life.

Your Mental Attitude

W. Clement Stone and Napoleon Hill, noted in the field of motivational literature, offered seventeen principles of success.

Writing about those in *Believe and Achieve,* Samuel A. Cypert said that list must be headed by having a positive mental attitude, for that has helped millions to take charge of their lives, realize their potential, and reach the lofty goals they have set for themselves.

A positive mental attitude is composed of faith, optimism, hope, integrity, initiative, courage, generosity, tolerance, tact, kindness, and good sense.

It is the most personal of principles. You — and you alone — can control what your mind accepts or rejects. You know that you face a barrage of negative influences every day. But you can replace those negative, self-defeating thoughts with positive, self-fulfilling thoughts.

Practice Daily

It's not always easy. You must practice it during every waking hour until it becomes a habit to greet self-doubt with self-confidence. You must have goals, develop self-confidence, and know that you are going to succeed.

Cypert promises that when you do this, the result is mind-boggling. You will find that you have unleashed a powerful force that will allow you to achieve any goal that you set for yourself.

Chapter 3

Creativity: Open Your Mind

Once you know where you want to go, there are several abilities you can develop to speed you on your way.

One that's often overlooked is creativity. Most people think of creativity as the province of artists, but there is room for creativity in all walks of life. Learn to open your mind and take advantage of your experience and abilities. You then will be better able to recognize and maximize opportunities and to turn problems into solutions.

If you develop your creativity, you'll be welcomed by businesses who know the premium that today's competitive firms put on discovery and initiative.

The individual creativity is **SPIRITED,** says William C. Miller in *The Creative Edge*. It's based on key strengths in at least some of the following characteristics:

Spontaneous: fresh, curious, willing to take risks, sense of humor.

Persistent: energetic, courageous, assertive, independent, determined.

Inventive: looks at problems in new ways, likes challenges, sometimes skeptical, comfortable with ambiguity.

Rewarding: willing to share credit, values personal satisfaction and peer recognition over money.

Inner openness: intuitive, easily switches from logic to fantasy, open to emotions, think/act/create/innovate in different modes.

Transcendent: sees situations realistically, fantasizes how he or she wants things to be, is confident he or she can effect change, chooses growth over fear.

Evaluative: discerning, discriminating, judgmental at appropriate times.

Democratic: values and respects people, seeks stimulation from variety of people, responsible, promotes highest benefits of all concerned.

Key Characteristics

Courage to take risks and persistence are the key characteristics of the creative person. The other characteristics are repeated patterns of thinking, feeling, and behaving.

We become that which we dwell on and to which we give our attention. So focus attention on yourself in your most creative moments. Imagine yourself as the creative person you want to be.

Start with a vision of who you are and want to be rather than what you want to do or have. You can build in the "doing" and "having" to fill out your vision.

Enhancing Creativity

While we're all creative, it may take some effort to bring out that creativity. Miller offers seven activities in which things "appear" to get created. He calls this the **APPEARE** process.

A Be AWARE of your complete current situation. For a scientist, that means analyzing the available facts and research. For a meeting planner, it could be who will attend and what will be covered. Keep your mind open. Useful information can come from unexpected sources.

P Be PERSISTENT in your vision. A persistent vision must be specific. Imagine it with all your senses. Focus on it often and positively, acknowledging doubts without investing energy in holding on to them. A writer may have a vision of a completed book, an entrepreneur a vision of a thriving business.

P PERCEIVE all your alternatives. Avoid "idea killers," people who make you feel impractical, stupid, or unsuccessful.

E ENTERTAIN your intuitive guidance. Relax so you can assimilate information and envision solutions. Your intuitive self compiles verbal and non-verbal information, then your muse takes over.

A ASSESS and select from among your alternatives. Sort them by category and rank them by criteria. Then choose combinations of solutions and eliminate unacceptable alternatives. Look for the best solution for all those affected, based on your emotions, intuition, and analysis. Don't let your ego tie you into a pet solution or a hidden agenda.

R Be REALISTIC in your actions. Act on the best knowledge available, then go with the results. Each result will stimulate more creativity and problem-solving for the next situation.

E EVALUATE your results. The creative process demands answers to the questions "Has the vision been realized? What are the results? What still needs to happen?" You can measure success by how well you foster an open, questioning environment for ideas or develop and document new ideas worth testing or accomplish positive results using documented innovative approaches.

Creativity is more than an act or a skill or a style of working. It's a way of being and of benefitting society.

Have Better Ideas

Creativity is a matter of unlocking the ideas that are within each of us, say Jimmy Calano and Jeff Salzman in *CareerTracking*.

Your inner voice, the subconscious mind, is at work when the conscious mind is doing something else. Learn to listen for that voice. When insights hit, turn your attention to them. Write them down immediately.

Break out of your thinking patterns. Try putting your problems on paper — by drawing them. Or snap yourself into a creative mood by doing your thinking in a different location — in an airplane or driving home by a different route.

Look for Answers

Look for more answers. Once you've thought of a "right" answer, try to think of three or four more. Something better usually surfaces.

Enlist the help of others. Write out the facts of a problem and your solutions. Then circulate these to those who work with you, from entry-level clerks to top management, anyone who might have an opinion. Set up brainstorming sessions.

Open yourself up to new and more ideas wherever and however you can.

Chapter 4

Listen and Learn

Tom Peters *(Thriving on Chaos)* puts it succinctly. If you want to foster involvement in the team concept in management, you have to listen constantly, share ideas and information, recognize achievement, and celebrate the small victories in day-to-day performance.

Emphasize listening, he says. It means paying attention to subordinates, teammates, and others. It can be informal, such as at a coffee break, or it can be formal, a planned meeting, complete with an agenda.

But listening isn't that simple — and it's a skill few people think of developing. It is such a routine, everyday activity that most people give it little or no thought. Yet it can have a tremendous impact on success in your personal and business life.

When you know how to really listen, you gain a strong advantage in your ability to acquire and retain knowledge. Listening is also a key factor in understanding and influencing other people.

Listen Better

"All of us can learn to listen better," says Thomas E. Anastasi Jr., in *Listen!*

Listening is getting meaning from situations involving the spoken word. The more familiar you are with words people use, the less often you need to interrupt the speaker to ask for clarification.

Listening can also tell us what people fear. It makes us aware of how we may unintentionally threaten and intimidate others.

Before we can deal with people, it helps to know their motivations, fears, and goals. We learn by listening.

Listening Is Hard Work

Listening can be more tiring than talking. That's because it demands intellectual, perhaps even emotional, effort. It's draining and tiring because — unlike hearing — it demands total concentration. Listening is an active search for

meaning while hearing is passive. When you listen, two people are thinking —
you and the speaker.

Focus on Listening

Words spoken to you come at the rate of 90 to 200 a minute. The differential between the speech and speed of thought explains why we are so easily distracted. The plodding speaker is using only a fraction of our listening capacity. With the rest of that capacity, our mind wanders.

You will concentrate better if you listen with questions in your mind. Evaluate, process, and use incoming information. Ask yourself:

- What's the speaker saying?
- What does it mean?
- How does it relate to what was said before?
- What point is the speaker trying to make?
- How is this helpful?
- How can I use the information the speaker is giving me?
- Does it make any sense?
- Am I getting the whole story?
- Are the points being backed up?
- How does this relate to what I already know?

You should also question the speaker, given the opportunity. The speaker will then perceive you as someone helping to develop the meaning in the situation. You and the speaker need to become partners in the exchange of meaning.

To Listen Better

Words have definitions but meaning comes from the people you're listening to. Feeling and emotion are part of that meaning. Being a good listener doesn't mean you have to be a psychologist, but it does mean you should be alert to the full dimension of meaning — not just words. To do this, you may have to help the speaker get the meaning across through your clarifying questions and by acquainting the speaker with your listening level.

Maintaining eye contact and an appropriate nod or two also help to let the speaker know you're listening.

Evaluation, positive or negative, affects the meaning a speaker will give you. To get into the speaker's mind, withhold evaluation until after the speaker has finished.

Be Patient and Paraphrase

One of the best ways to get people to listen to you is to listen to them. This may mean waiting for them to finish what they have to say.

Paraphrasing is another effective skill. When you paraphrase, you check your understanding of meaning, and show the speaker you have listened accurately.

Paraphrase when you want to make sure you've understood, when you're not sure you've caught the meaning, or before you agree or disagree. The paraphrase is also useful in dealing with people who repeat themselves. They need this assurance that they have communicated their ideas to you.

Phillip L. Hunsaker and Anthony J. Alessandra offer these tips for "power listening" in *The Art of Managing People:*

- Don't interrupt
- Listen for main ideas
- Concentrate on substance, not style
- Fight distractions
- Stifle anger
- Take brief notes
- Let others talk first
- Empathize
- Withhold judgment
- React to the message
- Read the feelings between the lines
- Ask questions.

Chapter 5

Effective Speaking

Those who speak well in public are more likely to be promoted than those who can't. Jeffrey P. Davidson calls this a "simple fact of career marketing," and in the summary of his book, *Blow Your Own Horn,* he says those who want to move ahead should practice speaking, even if their public appearances are limited to presentations at company meetings.

Preparation

To be a success, he says, you must be well prepared. As a starter, try to sum up in one sentence what message you want to leave with your audience. Often this will clarify your thinking.

Tackle only two or three ideas for one speech. To offer more means there's a strong chance your audience will forget all of them. And to make certain your audience doesn't forget, use anecdotes and examples to drive home those points.

Work for a strong opening statement. Figures may help to make it strong, but don't use too many of them or the audience will be lost.

Don't write out your speech. Outline it, using key words to remind you of your points. Practice, writing down only those key words to remind you of the sequence of your points. You won't express yourself the same way every time. Don't worry. It's better if you can tailor your delivery for your audience.

Work for a strong dynamic closing. One approach is to use an anecdote or example that will draw together the points you made.

After you've done your best to perfect your speech, try taping it. As you play it back, listen particularly to the pitch of your voice (keep it low) and the speed of delivery (not too fast).

Your Delivery

To be effective, you must believe in your message and its importance to your audience. If you must use note cards, place them on the table or podium, rather than holding them. Feel free to move away from the podium. You'll seem more dynamic if you move around.

Maintain eye contact with some individual in the audience through each thought. Your tone will be more conversational, and you'll be better able to read the response of your audience.

The Experts Say . . .

The specialists in speech agree on two points, and they are points frequently ignored by even experienced speakers.

● Don't write a speech, then read it. Maggie Bedrosian, author of *Speak Like a Pro,* says people want to hear you speak, not read. And unless you have a television prompter to help you, you'll find it very difficult to both read and look your audience in the eye — and looking at the audience is a must if you hope to sell them on your message.

● Don't try to memorize a speech, word by word. You'll sound as if you were reciting it, concentrating on the words of the speech, not on your message. And if you forget the words or get confused about where you are — disaster.

Getting Experience

The ability to speak comes only with practice. With each speech you make, you'll suffer less, and your message will be clearer and more effective.

You need speaking engagements to get that practice before an audience. Here's how to do it. First, prepare yourself to speak on three to five topics that will be of interest to many organizations. Davidson says that his first list included such topics as "Starting a New Venture" and "Light and Lively Management."

Type a one-page letter describing your background and listing those topics on which you are ready to speak. Make a list, from announcements in your paper, of organizations that meet. Learn who the program directors are, call them, then mail them your letter, and follow up with another phone call.

When you have a speech request, get some additional information before making your speech. You should know the size of the meeting room and its lighting, the seating arrangement, expected audience, program length, other speakers, and who will introduce you. If you plan to show slides, ask whether you will have to run the projector, and what type of projector, if any, is available.

Six Secrets of Speaking Success

W. Clement Stone says that to be a success, a speaker must act enthusiastic. Do this and soon you'll feel enthusiastic. To achieve this, Stone suggests these rules for speaking success:

1. Talk loudly, especially if you have "butterflies in your stomach."
2. Talk rapidly.
3. Emphasize words that are important to you or your listeners.
4. Modulate your pitch and volume.
5. Hesitate after words you wish to emphasize.
6. Keep a smile in your voice by putting one on your face and in your eyes.

Chapter 6

Managing Your Reading

The volume of reading that is essential today in most managerial positions is discouraging — but essential. To keep up, to know what is developing in the organization and within the area of your business, you must do a lot of reading. The answer is to be able to read faster and at the same time remember more from what you have read. But how to do it?

Some practical techniques are offered by Phyllis A. Miller, Ph.D., a reading specialist, in *Managing Your Reading*.

Pacesetting

Use your choice of two aids to help you to build up your reading speed as you move across the lines of print and down the page.

One aid is your hand, and most people use their right hand. Begin by placing your hand palm down on the page in a relaxed manner. Use your middle finger to lead you along underneath each line of type. Don't go all the way to the edge of the printed column. Stop when you are about one-half of an inch from the edge on the right, then move your hand down one line and to a half-inch from the edge on the left. Keep the tips of your fingers in contact with the page at all times. Move your hand as if you were underlining the words you are reading. This keeps your attention directed to that spot, and results in better concentration.

The second pacesetter aid is an unlined index card. Place it one or two lines above the line you are reading, so it doesn't get in your way. The card will push you along as you read and will discourage backtracking, which is often both habitual and unnecessary.

Use either your hand or the card to set various paces to build up your rate of reading. At first, simply try them out, reading at your normal pace. You will probably find they disrupt your concentration. They will become helpful only when you are less conscious of them.

Warm-up Pacing

Use warm-up pacing to get accustomed to higher speeds of reading. Set a pace considerably faster than you comfortably read, and keep it, regardless of your level of understanding of the material being read. At this point, comprehension has a low priority.

Efficient-rate Pacing

Efficient-rate pacing is reading for ideas as you pace with either your hand or a card. Concentrate on picking up the meaning as you go along. If you have done enough warm-up pacing, your pacing aid should move fairly automatically, and this will help you to read at a faster rate than you would without the aid.

After you have completed a passage — a page or so — check yourself. Without looking back at what you have just read, try to jot down phrases or sentences about the passage. Write them down, then go back over the reading to double-check your accuracy.

Measure Your Pacing Rate

Try these two methods to measure your reading rate:

1. One is the "eyeball" method. Simply look to see how much you have read, measuring in pages and fractions of pages when reading a book.

2. The other is the WPM (words per minute) method. First, get the average number of words in a line of print by counting three lines, then dividing by three. If the answer doesn't come out even, round down. Then, count the number of lines you read in a minute. Multiply this number by the average number of words in a line and you get the words per minute. (Six words per line times fifty lines equals 300 words per minute.)

Skimming

Skimming allows you to get the main ideas as you skip other parts of the material. It helps you to follow the writer's thinking and to see the development of each point. It shows you how to filter material as you move through it so that you pass over the lengthy discussions, examples, and fillers.

In skimming, you're trying to follow the writer's train of thought to get the main ideas. Read the introductory material in a chapter. This may be a single paragraph or a page or more.

Then read the first one or two sentences of the rest of the paragraphs. Try to determine the topic sentence, the one that contains the main idea of the paragraph. This is usually the first sentence of the paragraph.

Key Concept Words

Key concept words express the leading ideas of the material. As an example, in a book on public speaking, the word "communication" might be a key concept word, one to look for as you skim. Read sentences that contain key signal words, wherever they are found.

Key signal words signal emphasis, a shift in thought or a way of connecting one idea to another. They help the writer to develop the train of thought or to string the main ideas together.

Look for these key signal words at the beginning of a sentence or at the beginning of the second part of a compound sentence.

How to Skim

To prepare for skimming, analyze the book and the chapter titles to identify the key concept words.

Use your hand or a card as a guide, as we suggested earlier, reading only the first sentence of a paragraph. If you lose your train of thought, try backing up and also reading the last sentence of the preceding paragraph. Sometimes an author makes a point at the end of a paragraph, then refers to it in the next paragraph.

If the author switches to narrative to illustrate a point, you have a choice. Read it or skip it.

Skim slowly when you start new material. Get a feel for the author's style and the line of thought. Build up speed after you are more sure of what you are getting from the material.

Use skimming to approach difficult material you might otherwise avoid. It permits you to become acquainted with the material without dealing with details either prematurely or at all.

Chapter 7

Make the Best Decisions

Do you wince and hope someone else takes action when a decision must be made?

If your answer is yes, you're not alone. We're all faced with many decisions every day, ranging from what to have for lunch to selecting a new product for manufacturing. Many of us freeze when faced with decisions, even small ones. We're afraid of making the wrong choice.

If you're one of those who hate to make decisions, you are sure of one thing. This inability can halt a career dead in its tracks.

There is something you can do about it. You can gain confidence in your ability to make decisions and make the process easier and more likely to be successful.

Various step-by-step approaches to decision-making have been developed. One is put forth by Theodore Isaac Rubin, M.D., in *Overcoming Indecisiveness*.

Dr. Rubin notes that most of us are abdicators, not decision-makers, and we're not even aware of how we abdicate, or sometimes even that we abdicate. We just wait for things to happen instead of making them happen. We doubt or criticize decisions we're committed to, and we turn away from goals we know we could achieve. The result is enormous unhappiness, multiple failures in life, opportunities lost, deep frustrations, endless procrastination, and abiding hopelessness.

Worst of all, many don't even realize that they have this problem. They think all people react the way they do to making a decision.

The Choice You Make

Here's what Dr. Rubin calls the Big Fact: In few instances is one decision better than another.

That takes some explaining. We have options when we must make a decision. Few of them would be bad decisions, and few are discarded for that reason. We discard an option when we withdraw ourselves from it. By the same token, an option becomes a decision when we invest ourselves in it.

And what makes a decision work? It is almost always the decision-maker, and not the choice, that makes it work. Any failure has little to do with the choice. It is directly traceable and proportional to lack of dedicated commitment. Choices are good only if we make them good.

The first essential of the successful decision is to make that decision. The act of making a decision is almost always more important than the substance of the decision itself. Conversely, making no choice — indecision — invalidates all options because it paralyzes the victim. But the more we make decisions, the more natural the process becomes.

Steps of Decision-making

Studying the following eight steps of decision-making can help you if you're having difficulties. They will enable you to recognize your blockage and problems. That knowledge alone can help to break through the inertia of a blockage.

Usually we go through all or most of these steps without being aware of them, when we're making a decision. But they are there, regardless of the speed with which we arrive at a decision.

To become fully aware of the process of decision-making, we'll look at the process, not as it actually occurs, but in eight steps in slow motion.

1. We list our options. Judgment plays no role now. That would only impede creativity. We simply want to make up a list, no matter how ridiculous our options may look later. We want to let the unconscious freely come up with ideas, no matter how disconnected they may seem.

People who find choice difficult won't enjoy discovering they do have options, options that may appear as burdensome additions to their inner conflict. These people normally create very short lists.

That should signal to them that they have a problem; insight in this enormously important first phase is crucial to resolving the problem.

2. We think about our choices. That means sorting out our feelings about them. We find it hard to feel anything about some, so they're probably not worth our attention. Remember, though, this is not logical analysis. We're simply letting our thoughts come as they will, much in the way we thought about our options.

3. We observe our feelings. We're comfortable with some options, uncomfortable with others. Some seem "good," some seem wrong. We're now applying judgment to them. Careful here — don't rush to a conclusion. That results in impulsive decisions, which are, of course, pseudodecisions. Be patient and take your own feelings seriously. Don't worry about other people's. If you do, you'll have a hard time on this step. And make sure you go through this step. To skip it indicates poor self-esteem and sometimes hopelessness.

4. We relate our choices to our priorities. We create a list of priorities for each question requiring a decision. We jot down the list, then put our options against it. If you have well-established priorities, this will be easy. If you don't, take extra time here, and note that now you're coming very close to a decision.

5. We designate our choice. This proceeds smoothly from the previous step. Most often our choice sneaks up on us before we realize we've made a decision. Things should fall together, and we should feel good about ourselves and what we want. This strengthens our confidence in ourselves, strengthens our identity.

6. We register the decision. We let it become part of us. We discard the other options, let them drift away. We are "getting it all together" in preparation for action. We aren't backtracking. The obsessive ruminators have trouble at this stage, prolonging it beyond any practical value. They sit and sit, returning over and over to step three, until the final choice never is a true decision.

7. We commit to the decision. We don't drag our feet, look back, wonder. Choice becomes decision when implementation takes place. We focus time, energy, self, and purpose on the decision. If we can't, if we still think about alternatives, our indecision is sustained because we can't surrender those unchosen options. Our difficulty occurred at the fourth through the seventh step.

8. We help ourselves in every way possible to make our decision work. Other decisions might have worked just as well, but we are loyal to and optimistic about this one. It's ours. We're going to give it the utter loyalty that is characteristic of successful enterprise. Those who suffer from self-hate will show it here. They'll have difficulty sustaining either loyalty or optimism. They will abandon a decision at any sign of difficulty and become pessimistic about the choice. People with poor self-esteem will handle the first seven steps fairly well, then fail on this one.

If you take a specific question through these eight steps and reach a decision, you will accomplish a lot. You will understand that real decisions are possible only when we know what we feel. You will sense that the process of coming to a real decision is a healthy and satisfying one, a creative one. Successful experience with the decision process is the best way to become a successful decision-maker. Perhaps you've broken through some of those blocks that troubled you in the past, whether you know it or not.

Decision-thinking

Decision-making is just one stage in a mental process, say Ben Heirs and Peter Farrell in *The Professional Decision Thinker*. What they call decision-thinking is well-managed, rigorous, and imaginative. It's part of a process that begins with identifying problems and ends only when decisions have been carried out.

With practice, the four-stage decision-thinking process will become automatic.

Stage 1, the Question. Formulate a question that addresses the issue in the clearest possible way, without sacrificing any of its subtlety or complexity.

then gather information relevant to answering that question.

Stage 2, the Alternatives. Create many alternative answers to that question.

Stage 3, the Consequences. Evaluate each of the alternatives that emerge from Stage 2 by thinking through their implications and predicting the likely, as well as the possible, consequences. This prepares you to make a decision in the next stage and allows for hedging and contingency plans to be created in case that choice proves to be partially or wholly wrong.

As you approach the final stage, don't be too cautious. Don't be paralyzed by the fear of making a wrong decision, or procrastinate in the hope that it will be possible for you to prove without question that one choice is better than another.

Check Yourself

Before you start this vital final stage, run a quick check:

✔ Has the right question been asked in the most complete and richest way?

✔ Have all credible alternatives been considered?

✔ Have all possible consequences of each alternative been imagined and thought through?

✔ Have all foreseeable contingencies been provided for, as far as possible?

Next, weigh these factors in each possible course of action:

● *The estimated probability that it will be successful.*

A probability is never a certainty. Express it as a percentage — a 70 percent chance that something will work. That means there's a 30 percent chance that it won't — and that calls for contingency planning, deciding what you will do if it doesn't work.

● *The balance between the risk involved and the reward predicted.*

For example, the chances of a new product succeeding are rated at 85 percent. If your company could increase its profits by 20 percent in two years, but risks losing 5 percent of profits, the balance between risk and rewards favors you. But the balance doesn't if the cost of failure is 50 percent of annual profits.

The factors in any decision can be expressed this way as a set of equations in which risk is balanced against reward. But you can't make the decision on a purely mathematical basis, since that decision will depend on how urgently you desire the reward and how much you can afford to risk.

In the final analysis, the calculus of decision-thinking involves a balance of uncertainty. No decision can be reduced to a set of black and white issues. You must choose between a number of shades of gray. And now — the final stage.

Stage 4, the Decision. Weigh the probabilities of succeeding with each alternative, measure the balance between risk and reward offered by each alternative, then use judgment to make the decision.

This process is time-consuming and exhausting when applied to a complex problem. It demands a wide range of thinking techniques and skills. But it is this process, and only this process, that will give us the chance to think our way wisely into the future.

Decision-thinking, however well it is practiced, doesn't guarantee infallibility. But if it is executed professionally, it can tip the odds in favor of making a good decision, and those odds are what our practical life is all about.

Make Fast Decisions

Jimmy Calano and Jeff Salzman take a slightly different look at decision-making in *CareerTracking*. They say it's more important to be decisive than to be right. This is because decisiveness inspires support and intimidates the opposition, who think you know something they don't. In competitive circumstances, a not-so-great decision made quickly can have better results than a good decision made slowly.

In business, they say, 80 percent of your decisions should be made on the spot, 15 percent need to mature, and 5 percent need not be made at all.

Peter Drucker, management specialist, says, "People who don't take risks generally make about two big mistakes a year. People who do take risks generally make about two big mistakes a year."

Be Confident

Present your decision confidently in the spirit of "let's try this," but be ready to change any decision to cut your losses. For most decisions, you can't get all the facts, so respect your hunches. They're usually a result of accessing the vast knowledge and experience in your subconscious mind.

Don't, however, wing it on big decisions where the knowledge of an expert like an accountant or lawyer can be helpful. A quick call can minimize your risk.

Chapter 8

Managing Your Stresses

The pressures of life, and especially life on the job, create stress for most people. And, says Marvin Karlins in *The Human Use of Human Resources,* learning to manage stress can make a strong positive contribution to your success and your personal well-being.

Stress is not necessarily bad. Moderate amounts can even enhance a person's performance. This "good" stress can almost be a "high." It is the type of stress that a marathon runner is under as he pushes himself to complete the full twenty-six miles of the run. Anyone who pushes to achieve a goal knows what a tremendous "high" successful completion produces.

"Good" stress contributes to attaining goals and achieving more than you ever thought possible. "Bad" stress is created when stress itself becomes excessive. Continually placing a mind and body under stress eventually leads to lapses in judgment, reduction of creativity, nervous breakdowns, heart attacks, and even death.

Defeating Stress

The relaxation response, pioneered by Dr. Herbert Benson and Mariam Klipper, is a form of meditation by which the meditator strives to achieve a state of "restful alertness" by spending two twenty-minute periods each day in "comfortable isolation," letting the mind empty of all thoughts and distractions.

Not only has the relaxation response been effective in defeating the mental side of stress, but there is also much evidence that a person reaps many physiological benefits from such meditation.

Among those benefits are a lower respiratory rate, decreased oxygen consumption, diminishing heart rate, and in some hypertensive individuals, decreased blood pressure. The relaxation response has also been shown to alleviate dependence on drugs, alcohol, and tobacco.

How to Try It

Simple steps make it possible for anyone, anywhere, to achieve the response.

First, sit quietly in a comfortable position. Close your eyes. Relax all your muscles, beginning at your feet and progressing up to your face. Keep them relaxed.

Breathe easily and naturally, and through your nose unless this is uncomfortable. As you breathe, say "one" to yourself. For example, breathe in . . . out, "one," in . . . out, "one," in . . . out, "one."

Continue this for twenty minutes. You may open your eyes to check the time, but do not use the alarm of a clock to time yourself. When you finish, sit quietly for several minutes, at first with your eyes closed and later with your eyes open. Do not stand for a few minutes.

Don't worry about achieving a deep level of relaxation. Permit relaxation to occur at its own pace. When distracting thoughts occur, try to ignore them. Return to repeating "one." With practice the response should come with little effort.

Practice the technique twice daily, but not within two hours after any meal, since the digestive processes seem to interfere with achieving the relaxation response.

The response will not only help to combat excessive stress, but will also enhance alertness and job performance.

Defeating Stress Physically

One of the best ways to beat excessive stress is to live an active life, and effective exercise is an important aspect of it.

To be effective, exercise must be aerobic. Aerobic exercises involve sustained activity that stimulates the heart and lungs long enough to produce beneficial changes in the body. Brisk walking, jogging, swimming, cycling, and skipping rope are aerobic exercises.

For those exercises to be effective, plan on spending at least twenty minutes each day, at least four to six days a week, on them. Exercising less than this will not produce the optimum effects.

Chapter 9

Avoid Burnout

Closely linked to stress in the minds of many is burnout, a popular term that has grown to include such conditions as job dissatisfaction, depression, and alienation.

Ayala Pines and Elliot Aronson are more specific in their definition of burnout in their book, *Career Burnout*. It is, they say, a state of physical, emotional, and mental exhaustion caused by long-term involvement in situations that are emotionally demanding. Burnout candidates are idealists who chose a career in which they thought they could make a difference. Instead, they find themselves running into chronic situational stresses.

People who suffer burnout exhibit an array of symptoms — physical depletion and feelings of helplessness, hopelessness, and disillusion. They develop a negative concept of themselves and negative attitudes toward their work, those involved in the work, and even life itself. In the most extreme form, those suffering from burnout reach a breaking point beyond which their abilities to cope with the environment is severely hampered.

Costs Are High

Burnout can be costly, for both individuals and companies. Burned-out workers have lower morale, higher absenteeism and tardiness, and greater turnover. They develop negative attitudes toward themselves and their work and become detached, contemptuous, or callous toward customers, clients, and colleagues.

The recruiting, hiring, and training costs to replace burned-out workers who resign or who are only marginally productive are much higher than if the problems of those workers were acknowledged and they were rehabilitated.

Very successful executives are often victims of burnout. These are men and women to whom success at work is a primary goal.

That is closely linked with their problems that lead to burnout. After the thrill of success subsides, they tend to take success for granted. This dilutes its reward power. And they are haunted with the specter of failure, the voice within them asking, "What have you done lately?"

These same successful persons often lack total control over their work. They are frustrated by such things as inadequate authority, finances, or staff, they feel political pressure, are troubled by red tape, and conclude that they simply can't do their jobs the way they know it should be done.

Companies Can Help

Companies can do much to avoid burnout in the ranks of their employees.

At the psychological level, a company should design jobs to give employees a sense of significance and opportunities for personal growth. Workers should have a sense of autonomy and variety. Although they should be challenged and kept busy, workers shouldn't be buried under an avalanche of work.

Work conditions should be good, with effective lighting, comfortable furniture, and well-maintained equipment that's suitable for the job.

Don't Overload Employees

Employees shouldn't be assigned an overload of customers or clients. Work breaks and vacations should provide time off. Management, too, should provide adequate feedback, support, rewards, and challenge.

Companies that recognize some of their jobs are stressful can adopt a "time-out" work policy. This isn't an extra coffee break. It's a time when workers are shifted to do less stressful work while their colleagues take over the more stressful responsibilities. Similarly, managers can avoid assigning double shifts and frequent overtime work for employees on stressful jobs.

If burnout is a pressing company problem, firms should provide burnout education at seminars, conferences, and workshops. These activities give workers a chance to examine their work pressures, clarify their goals, and evaluate unused coping strategies.

What You Can Do

Begin by analyzing your personality. If you move rapidly, are impatient with the speed at which most events take place, want to hurry others, and try to do two things at once, such as dictating while driving, you have a Type A personality, and you may be showing some of the symptoms of burnout.

As a starter, resolve to find a sense of importance in something besides work.

Develop New Interests

Develop an interest in the broader satisfactions of life. For example, take up a hobby or learn to play a musical instrument. Take time — make time — to smell the roses.

Set goals for both your work and your private life. These goals should give purpose and meaning to your life.

Place your job in perspective and keep it there. Appraise the value of other facets of your life, including your spouse, children, friends, and hobbies. See employment as only one source of satisfaction and significance, and identify others.

If your company provides self-enrichment courses, opportunities to attend conventions, in-service classes, or leaves of absence, take advantage of them.

Reappraise your long-term and short-term goals. Unrealistic goals and expectations virtually guarantee failure. Then jot down the changes you want to make in your daily life, how much power you have to make those changes, and what alternatives you might pursue.

How Burned Out Are You?

You can compute your burnout score by completing the following questionnaire. How often do you have any of the following experiences? Please use the scale in rating yourself.

1	2	3	4	5	6	7
Never	Once in a great while	Rarely	Sometimes	Often	Usually	Always

_____   1. Being tired.

_____   2. Feeling depressed.

            3. Having a good day.   _____

_____   4. Being physically exhausted.

_____   5. Being emotionally exhausted.

            6. Being happy.   _____

_____   7. Being "wiped out."

_____   8. "Can't take it any more."

_____   9. Being unhappy.

_____ 10. Feeling run down.

_____ 11. Feeling trapped.

_____ 12. Feeling worthless.

_____ 13. Being weary.

_____ 14. Being troubled.

_____ 15. Feeling disillusioned, resentful.

_____ 16. Being weak, susceptible to illness.

_____ 17. Feeling hopeless.

_____ 18. Feeling rejected.

           19. Feeling optimistic.   _____

           20. Feeling energetic.   _____

_____ 21. Feeling anxious.

Figure your score ⇩

Figure Your Score

1. Add the values you wrote next to the following items
   (left column):
   1, 2, 4, 5, 7, 8, 9, 10, 11, 12, 13, 14, 15, 16, 17, 18, 21   _____
2. Add the values you wrote next to the following items
   (right column):
   3, 6, 19, 20   _____
3. Subtract that number from 32:   32 − _____ = _____
4. Add your answers in steps 1 and 3   _____
5. Divide this number by 21. This is your burnout score: _____

What It Means

- If your score is between 2 and 3, you are doing well. (Were you honest in your responses?)
- If your score is between 3 and 4, you should examine your work and life, evaluate your priorities, and consider possible changes.
- If your score is higher than 4, you are experiencing burnout. Do something about it.
- If your score is higher than 5, you are in an acute state and need immediate help.

PART II

HOW TO MAKE THE MOST OF YOUR CAREER

Personal and career skills overlap a great deal, but certain skills are particularly valuable for gaining control of your destiny and putting your best foot forward on the job.

The first section of this part deals with what may be the most critical career skill: getting organized. You'll find expert advice on how to make every hour of the work day count by spending more time on important, productive matters. And you'll learn how to make the telephone an ally, rather than an enemy, in time management.

Reduce Paperwork

One of the best ways to get organized is to reduce the amount of paperwork you create and receive, and to handle what's left systematically. The approaches presented should help you as you develop a system that fits your needs.

Another vital skill is communicating. This goes beyond public speaking, covered in the first part. It includes verbal and nonverbal techniques that will, over time, become habits that will boost your effectiveness and your career prospects.

Still another must for career advancement is making sure that others are aware of your abilities and achievements. You can only do that by selling yourself. This part offers a number of strategies and techniques that will help you to gain a place for yourself in the upper echelons of your business.

In today's fast-changing business world, the skills and strategies that used to guarantee success don't always work. This part concludes with skills for the future, a look at areas you'll want to develop for the years ahead.

Chapter 10

Get Organized

It's all too easy to get lost in the paperwork and interruptions that dominate many workdays. A disorganized approach to your work and life can leave you wondering at the end of each day what you accomplished — and knowing it wasn't much.

You won't get anywhere until you gain control of your time and tasks. You have to get organized and learn to manage your time, your paperwork, and even the telephone.

Time Management

The place to start is with time management. A concise outline of what you need to do is presented in *The Working Woman Report* by the editors of *Working Woman* with Gay Bryant. As you read this list, check the ones on which you should concentrate to improve your management of your time.

- Draw up a plan each day of what you want to accomplish.
- Develop daily, weekly, monthly, and yearly lists of goals.
- Set priorities, and learn to weigh yours against those of your boss. Don't passively accept a deadline you can't meet.
- Schedule hours for quiet work and other times when you will be available to other people.
- Never handle a piece of paper more than twice. Once is much better. Aim for that.
- Use technology — computers, calculators, phones.
- Cut down on business reading. Learn to skim.
- Attend only the most important meetings.
- Do business during coffee breaks and lunches.
- Exercise at least twenty minutes a day to clear your head and boost your energy.
- Delegate. Use your time and effort for those tasks that only you have the authority or skills to handle.

Get Focused

In *The Energetic Manager,* Fred Pryor offers some suggestions for getting a handle on your priorities and finding the time to complete your high-priority items.

Do you have trouble doing things simply because you can't seem to harness the time or the concentration? But, when it's something you enjoy, do you find time?

On the task that you enjoy, you don't procrastinate because you anticipate the sense of achievement you'll feel when the work is completed. You are working toward a clearly defined goal that stems from your values.

You must learn to gather the same excitement for less pleasant tasks by creating a clear and favorable picture of the end result. Focus on that result rather than the tedious or difficult steps leading up to it. Place a carrot in front of yourself.

Remember Priorities

Take a few minutes to analyze your workday. Do you find yourself reading unimportant material or answering equally unimportant phone calls when you should be tackling a project that you've been putting off for weeks? Do you find yourself, at the end of the day, unable to think of any true accomplishment?

If your answers were "yes," you're creating tremendous stress and anxiety for yourself, because you're feeling vulnerable and out of control.

What to do about it?

First, ask yourself, many times a day, "Is this the most important thing I could be doing right now?" Change if your answer is "no."

Daily 'To Do' List

Make a daily "To Do" list with items listed in order of importance. Check them off as you complete them. Add items if you do other things. You'll know, at the end of each day, what you accomplished and what you wasted time in doing.

(If your boss tends to heap work on you, this "To Do" list can serve another purpose. When asked to take on more work, pull out the list and say, "I'm willing to put in the additional hours of work, but which of these items would you like me to postpone so that I can do what you've just given me?")

Know Yourself

Are you a morning or an afternoon person? You should know, and schedule your work accordingly, with the important projects scheduled for when you are at your peak.

Most people function best from the time they get to work to about 11, think of food or are lethargic after eating until about 1:30, then swing back to better work until quitting time. Schedule your work and your meetings to take advantage of the time when you function best. Avoid late afternoon meetings, however. People's tempers and attention span are short at that time.

Learn to Say 'No'

Interruptions can be one of the biggest problems you face in managing time. The phone rings. An employee drops in. If you give in to such interruptions, you'll be wasting valuable time, dissipating your energy, and frustrating yourself by your lack of achievement.

Prevent this by learning to say "no." If you're working on a deadline, say "no" or "later" to the drop-in guest.

Adopt a "screen-door policy" instead of an "open-door policy." Ask your secretary to screen all calls and guests, interrupting you only when it is necessary.

Help your staff to become independent by asking them, before they bring you a problem, to write out the problem, suggest three possible solutions, and identify the best solution of the three. Often they'll realize they don't need to see you, or they only need an OK on the solution.

Gain Control

"To do" lists and techniques for establishing priorities are among the ways to gain control of your workday, says Stephanie Winston in *The Organized Executive*.

However you do it, your aim is to refocus and harness the time you can control, and minimize the impact of the demands you can't control.

Gaining control requires you to:

● Define what you have to do and when you should do it.

● Develop strategies for defending your schedule against interruptions, time wasters, and procrastination, and find the most efficient ways to do what you have to do.

● Evaluate your daily activities against your aspirations, in order to organize your time so that you can realize your long-term goals.

Make Lists

Planning your workday requires you to make two basic lists, a comprehensive Master List and a specific Daily List.

The Master List is a single, continuous list, kept in a notebook, of every single thing you have to do, big or little, right away or in six months. The list quantifies your workload.

To use this list, you must distribute and schedule the items in it so they actually get done. Thus you must review it daily, deleting anything unnecessary or finished. You should also break down complicated tasks into components, so that you can schedule each component.

Delegate

Refer all tasks that can be delegated to staffers and cross them off, using your calendar or tickler file for follow-ups. Schedule action dates for long-term tasks, transfer them to your calendar, and cross them off. Then select the items that require immediate attention.

To work with the Daily List, late each afternoon draw it up for the follow-ing day. Put down the immediate tasks that have evolved during the course of the day, the previously scheduled calendar items that have become current, and those items from the Master List that require immediate attention.

A Daily List shouldn't include more than ten tasks. Limiting the list to ten items prevents the paralysis that can arise when your workload seems unmanageable.

Set Priorities

Since not all items on the Daily List are equal in importance, you must set priorities and match your commitment of time and resources to the relative importance of each task.

Do this by ranking each item on your Daily List as a 1, 2, or 3, according to these criteria:

1 is an immediate, "must-do" item, a task requiring special effort or concentration, or a stressful task, such as criticizing a subordinate's work.

2 is a middle-range item.

3 is routine busy-work, such as reading a journal.

Never schedule more than three or four priority 1 items during a day, because you won't be able to do them all, and you will get frustrated. Also, don't increase the number of items on the Daily List to accommodate left-overs from previous days.

The Payoff/Priority Rating

Get in the habit of evaluating each item on your Daily List on the basis of its payoff — its contribution to your goals and responsibilities.

High-payoff items promise to yield substantial or dramatic benefits. Putting together a winning sales campaign would be one of these. There should be at least one high-payoff task on each Daily List, particularly since these items sometimes tend to get lost in the day-to-day surprises of "crisis management." Negative-payoff items are must-do's, because the consequences of not doing them are disastrous. Paperwork processing is such an item.

Medium-payoff items are the basic, day-to-day substance of your job. They are usually number 2 priorities.

Low-payoff items offer few benefits, positive or negative. They should rarely appear on your Daily List, and never with a priority higher than 3. One of your goals should be to get rid of them.

Control Your Time

You can't control your time without scheduling your workday. Otherwise, you will spend your day reacting to "crises," and end the day without having gotten even your top priority tasks accomplished.

Schedule those top priority tasks during your "personal prime time." This period, along with your daily paperwork sessions, are the fixed points in your daily schedule. The scheduling of the rest of the day depends on the kind of job you have and your own temperament.

Develop a schedule by first dividing your day into "public" and "private" activities. Public activities include "drop-in meetings," phone calls, and unexpected events. Private activities include paperwork, writing reports, and reading.

Select your most demanding activities and schedule them into your "prime-time" block. For some people, these will be private activities like writing. A sales rep might find them to be phone calls and other "public" activities. Schedule the less demanding tasks in blocks during your "lower" time. Read during your "slump."

Fingertip Management

Charles R. Hobbs is frank in his assessment: some managers can't even manage the tops of their desks.

Their goal is to have everything they need at their fingertips when they need it. Then they bury themselves in paper while trying to achieve this goal. Stacks of paper on the desk do create a sense of urgency, but they also tend to mix the vital and the trivial.

These managers also try to organize themselves with calendars. They have a large flat monthly calendar, one-sheet-per-day calendar, and a wall calendar. Then there's an expense book, phone directories, and a Rolodex, all at arm's length. Also close at hand are a pile of "to do" lists and tickler files.

The result: When they want to retrieve information, they go from one pile or calendar or file to another, wasting a lot of time.

Declare War

Declare war on this complexity and promise yourself that you will have a perfectly clean desk.

Start by throwing away all of the varied calendars and putting all of that information in a date book organizer.

The space you can reach from where you sit should contain only items you use very frequently, like that date book organizer.

Keep occasionally used items such as paper clips slightly out of reach. Files and other less frequently used papers should be placed several steps away in a filing cabinet. And some of those papers belong in the wastebasket.

Phone Location

Even the telephone shouldn't be right at hand unless you use it constantly; otherwise, its high visibility creates an unnecessary sense of urgency.

Instead of in-baskets and out-baskets claiming a lot of your desk top, use an in-drawer and an out-drawer. That takes the urgency out of that pile of paper. Inform the people who leave you things about the new arrangement.

Impressed with the new look of true fingertip management? Perhaps now it looks too much like an austere cell. A plant or pictures can bring beauty for you and for others.

Master the Time Wasters

The surest way to destroy your schedule is to allow the incessant demands of office life to go unchecked. You must defend your organized day by managing the interruptions and meetings that threaten to throw you off course.

The first necessity is to reduce interruptions. Since crises do arise, in even the best organized offices, it is simply not practical to shut yourself off completely for the whole day. In fact, this approach can shield you from problems until they become crises.

A more realistic approach is to limit the time you control fully to certain blocks, including your prime-time block and scheduled appointments, and to deal with the rest of the day more flexibly.

But the periods when you are available for questions and advice should not be free-for-alls. You should eliminate avoidable distractions and reduce the time spent on unavoidable ones.

Deal with Unexpected Visitors

Too much interoffice visiting can cause problems. One strategy for dealing with visitors is to put your secretary between you and them. Have her tell them you are busy. "Would you like me to interrupt him/her?" will deter all but the most nervy. If you don't have a secretary, a sign on the door indicating that you are working should help. If you can, do your private work elsewhere — at home, in the library, or in an empty conference room.

Consolidate visitors by scheduling appointments and meetings into a block of time. Set up regular meetings with staff and your secretary, if they are your most frequent visitors, and aim to cover all problems and questions at one session.

If you do need to confer, try to do it in a colleague's office, rather than your own. It's easier to leave than to ease someone out.

Procrastination

Sure, it's easy to blame others — demanding bosses, social co-workers, help-seeking staff members — for our inability to get things done.

But be honest. How often is it your own fault, that you simply put off doing what will still be in the in-box tomorrow?

Procrastination is rampant in the business world, says Sullivan. It affects both sexes, and people of all ages. It devastates personal relationships, causes emotional anguish, wrecks any attempt at effectiveness, and has probably ruined more careers than hard drinking.

Procrastinators are looked upon as easygoing and relaxed. They aren't. They are victims of stress at several levels, and the more they put off action, the more anxious they become. And they spread tension among those around them.

Do You Procrastinate?

Procrastinators are experts at self-delusion, so an honest answer by them to that question is difficult. A diary of your activities for a day, minute by minute, may show the answer. Do you watch TV at home just because it's on? In the office, do you shuffle papers? Do you wait for "just the right time" to do specific work?

Did you answer "yes" to any of those questions? If you did, welcome to the Loyal Order of Procrastinators.

If you want to turn in your LOP badge, there are things you can do to overcome this. Try at least one of these — today:

● Prepare daily "to do" lists. Each morning jot down what you want to accomplish that day. Establish priorities. Cross off each item as it is completed. You'll get a feeling of accomplishment from this that will help you to continue the system.

● Delegate. This is especially difficult for procrastinators because they feel that they are the only ones who can do the job.

● Divide big jobs into little ones. This is the best method for those whose goal is to complete tasks of earth-shaking proportions. Finishing a designated part of the task gives you that feeling of accomplishment and keeps you going on to the next step. The daily accomplishment adds up fast.

● Use self-exhortation. Talk like a Dutch uncle into a cassette recorder, urging yourself to do this or that task. Just making the tape will keep you going for some time. Then play it back from time to time, when you need a talking to by the world's foremost authority on you: yourself.

Chapter 11

The Phone: Friend or Foe?

The telephone can be a curse or a blessing in your quest to gain control of your time.

Robert Townsend in *Further Up the Organization* describes the phone as an underused tool.

When you need to talk to someone, don't assume it must be a face-to-face meeting, with a time and place set for it. Instead, pick up the phone. Do it quickly. This is instant communication and that can be valuable to both parties. The other person will be pleased that you took the trouble, that you didn't write a formal note, that the sound of your voice and not the clack of your typewriter is there. Best of all, there is instantaneous give and take.

But, as we all know, the phone can also be a major time waster. You can reduce that wasted time, says George Sullivan in *Work Smart, Not Hard*.

Prepare to Phone

Before you place a call, list the points you want to cover. When you have covered them with the person called, you may want to socialize briefly, but be ready to cut off the conversation when the opportunity rises. Try something like, "Gee, Gil, I know you must be busy. I can't take any more of your time."

If people you call never fail to be long-winded, stop calling them. Deal with them by letter or memo.

Friends who remain on the phone for a half-hour or more are probably using you as a substitute therapist, says Shirley Belz of the National Home Study Council. "Interject some of your own problems and you'll soon find they don't have time to talk."

Look for Improvement

Take advantage of the improvements in telephones. A cordless phone lets you walk around as you talk. A speaker phone enables you to work with your hands while handling a call. Automatic dialing can be a good time saver if you place a lot of calls. Automatic paging systems and beepers may solve some of your problems. Cellular phones make phoning while driving an easy matter, and they're available for your own car or in rental cars. Air-to-ground phone service from planes is getting more and more commonplace. At home, a phone answering machine or an answering service may be useful.

Have Calls Screened

If you have a secretary, ask to be shielded from as many calls as possible during "private" work periods and meetings, suggests Stephanie Winston.

Provide your secretary with a list of people to whom you will speak during those periods.

Try to have other people handle your calls whenever possible. If your secretary asks callers the purpose of the calls, she may be able to handle the problem or direct the caller to someone who can. Appoint staffers to handle all routine business with regular callers or clients, referring them to you only if a problem arises.

Handle your own calls efficiently. Consolidate them and make them during periods when other people are less inclined to chat, such as just before lunch. Develop a system for keeping track of call-backs. If there are many calls, a telephone log will be useful.

Organizing Audit

Do you want to know how well organized you are? Give the most honest answers you can to the questions following, then figure your score.

Scoring the Organizing Audit

Questions 1-7; 1 point for each "no." _____

Questions 8-19; 1 point for each "yes." _____

Add together for total score: _____

What does your score tell you?

Score 1-5: You are already a very well organized person.

Score 6-8: You are having difficulties.

Score 9-12: You are distinctly hampered by disorder.

Score 13-19: You need a full-fledged reorganization.

Organizing Audit

	YES	NO
1. Can you retrieve any paper from your desk within one minute?		
2. Can your secretary retrieve papers from the office files within five minutes of your request?		
3. When you walk into your office in the morning, do you know what your two or three primary tasks are?		
4. Do you usually accomplish those tasks that day?		
5. Do you meet daily with your secretary, and weekly with your staff?		
6. Does your staff typically receive clear-cut assignments that outline the range of their authority, the overall purpose, and the due date?		
7. Do you always monitor staff to ensure that tasks are completed on time?		
8. Are there some papers on your desk, other than reference material, that you haven't looked through for a week or more?		
9. During the last three months, have you failed to reply to an important letter because it was lost on your desk?		
10. Do you regularly receive letters or calls that begin, "You haven't gotten back to me yet, so . . .?"		
11. Within the last three months, have you forgotten any scheduled appointments or meetings, or any special dates that you wanted to acknowledge?		
12. Do you carry home a loaded briefcase more than once a week?		
13. Are you harassed by frequent interruptions — whether phone calls or visitors — that affect your ability to concentrate?		
14. Do you frequently procrastinate on an assignment until it becomes an emergency or panic situation?		
15. Do you receive long reports from which you have to extract a few key points?		
16. Do your own reports tend to be wordy or excessively detailed?		
17. Do magazines and newspapers pile up unread?		
18. Do you often wind up doing a little bit of your staff's jobs in addition to your own?		
19. Are you so busy with details that you are ignoring opportunities for new business activities?		

Chapter 12

Cut Back the Paperwork

Most of our technological advances in the world of the business office in recent years — the computer, the copying machine, the fast-printing shops, the modem, and the fax — enable us to turn out more and more paperwork faster and faster.

And we've learned to use them — with a vengeance.

One goal of the computer was to move toward communication in a paperless business society where words and figures passed from your monitor to mine without paper. But link that computer to a modern printer and it will spew forth words faster than they can be read.

Are we offering you a nostalgic plea to return to the good old days before Gutenberg? Is this a suggestion that we go back to a day — even before the use of the mimeograph machine and carbon paper — when so little paperwork could be produced by so many?

Of course not.

We're just issuing a warning. Your career, if you let it, can be buried beneath paper. To avoid this, you need a system that will quickly sort out what you need and move the remainder out of your way.

Stephanie Winston, in *The Organized Executive,* offers such a system. The key to managing the paper you receive, she says, is decision-making and processing.

The TRAF Technique

There are two things you can do with a piece of paper on your desk. You can avoid managing it by leaving it there to gather dust. Or you can TRAF it. TRAF is an acronym for the four decisions you can make about each piece of paper.

You can TOSS it in the wastebasket, REFER it to someone else, ACT on it, or FILE it. The only way to handle your paperwork successfully is to TRAF every single piece of it.

Toss. *Business Week* says, "Man's best friend, aside from the dog, is the wastebasket." If you hate to toss papers in the wastebasket, keep asking yourself what is the worst thing that could happen if you tossed them out. But don't agonize over this. If in doubt, keep it with other papers to be filed.

Refer. That means delegating the paper to a secretary or staffer, or passing it along to a colleague with greater knowledge or expertise in the area. Some of this can just be marked for a specific person and dropped into your out-box. If you wish to follow up on any of it, make up a personal track file, with folders marked for your secretary, your boss, and all reporting staff members. Drop a carbon of any assignment or idea in the person's folder, then once a week or so, review the files and ask for progress reports.

Act on it. Put all the papers that require action on your part into an "action" box or folder. Acts include writing a letter or report or doing research.

File it. Set up a folder marked "to file" for your own files. Put papers that go to the general office files in your out-box. Remember that if you have to do something with the paper, it's an "Action," not a "File."

Acting on the Action Pile

Once you've TRAFed every piece of paper on your desk, you're ready for the second half of the daily paper processing routine, and that's acting on the "Actions."

Start by moving all the follow-ups scheduled for today to the action stack. Then go through it and take out the two or three most urgent tasks. After taking care of these, work through the rest of the box as it falls. Do not shuffle pieces of paper around. Make a decision about each piece of paper you pick up.

Take each piece as far as you can go with it, or until it is ready to be referred to someone else. When you can't sign off on it right away, arrange to follow it up, as discussed below.

In this process, don't forget to TRAF your briefcase, which is a mode of transport, not a long-term storage facility.

Following Up

Keeping track of yourself and others is the essential flip side of the action process. You have to be sure that deadlines are met and commitments honored. Failure to follow up can produce not just disorganization, but disaster.

Memory is a very inefficient way of keeping track. Much more effective are calendar/holding files and tickler files.

In using the calendar/holding file, put each item in the file, then make a note on your calendar on the date you must follow it up. Keep jotting reminders on your calendar, and when the transaction is finally completed on the date chosen, recirculate the original papers by putting them through the TRAF process again.

A tickler file is needed if you have too many follow-ups to jot down on the calendar. Set up a file folder for each day of the current month, plus folders for each month, then put documents into the file for the date on which you must follow up. Each day, process the paper in that day's file.

Digging Out From Under

You should start the TRAF process by working through your first day's supply of paper. But once you've gotten this under control, you're ready to deal with the backlog, the papers that have piled up over the past few weeks, months, or years. If you have a lot, you might schedule two or three Saturday sessions — and have lots of trash bags ready for the Toss material.

If your desk is a pile of paperwork, start by dividing it into four sections, then clearing those sections , one at a time. TRAF each piece of paper in the first section until you reach the desk top. Then start on the second section.

Clear Out Drawers

Once your desk top is clear, clear out the drawers. Next, do any papers stacked elsewhere in your office.

Often this "dig out" will leave you with a massive Action box. Delegate as many of these papers as possible, and divide the remainder into two levels of priority, A and B. Integrate the A material gradually into your daily processing routine, until you are caught up. Then do the B material. Don't be dismayed if the whole process takes several weeks.

The Fine Art of Filing

If you don't know where to find a document, it might as well not exist. There is probably buried treasure in your file — ideas, information, business leads. The reason you can't find that treasure is because you don't have a map, a clearly defined classification system for your files.

An effective system is based on clear, simple categories that reflect your needs for information. There are three basic rules of file classification:

1. Use broad generic headings, based on your reason for keeping the papers. A note from a new business acquaintance may be a "Prospect" or a "Contact." If you file it under the person's name, it will be lost for good.

2. Use headings comprehensive enough to absorb a substantial quantity of papers. If your file drawers are full of skinny folders, you almost certainly have more headings than you can keep track of. The idea is to merge similar materials into a few "fat" files.

3. Head folders with a noun, not an adjective, adverb, date, or number. A list of new "hot" prospects will be lost forever if filed under "new" lists. Nobody will remember what the "new" meant.

Reduce the Load

You will reduce your workload if you cut back the amount of paper you must TRAF. Start by collecting a month's worth of reports, then analyzing them.

First, eliminate all reports that provide you with vital information you can get any other place. If you can't ask the originator of these reports to take you off the list, ask your secretary to discard them automatically.

Second, look at the remaining reports. Do you need to know everything in the report, or just sections of it? Get your assistant to flag the pertinent stuff, or to tear off the pages you need and toss the rest. If you can, get the report writers to provide you with summaries. You can always get more detailed information if you need it. If you can delegate certain reports directly to staff members, do so.

Get Some Help

Many other approaches to handling paperwork have been developed. George Sullivan suggests that you begin by having someone else sort what comes into your office, separating what you should see from what can be discarded or passed on to another person for action.

Then take the paper that ends up on your desk and divide it into five categories:

1. Urgent. Papers that demand immediate attention. If a decision is needed, make it. If a letter must be answered, dictate that answer. If a telephone call is needed, make it. Don't put off anything you decide is urgent.

2. Read and save. Put these papers in a folder, and read from the folder when you have time, such as when you're traveling. If the stack gets too large, schedule time for reading. As each item is read, mark it for filing or for action by a subordinate.

3. Read and discard. This is material of secondary importance, such as trade newspapers and magazines. If, after a week or two, you haven't read it, discard it. It has undoubtedly lost whatever importance it once had.

4. File. Make a note, if needed, telling where to file each item.

5. Discard. This should be the largest pile.

A common rule is to handle a paper only once. Most of us have tried this, and failed. Instead, make it a rule to do something that advances the project every time a particular paper is picked up. Failure to do this means you're going to have to pick up that paper again sometime in the future. That's not working smart.

Here's a way to test your effectiveness. Every time you pick up a paper, make a tiny check in the lower right corner of page one. When check marks begin to accumulate, it's a sign you're wasting time on the subject, and you must make a final decision.

Cutting Your Production

You may be contributing to the paper glut with your production of reports and other papers. Start by analyzing a month's worth of the reports you and your staff produce.

Judge them. Reports shouldn't be simply a collection of facts. They should provide the information in the right form so that people can use them to make decisions.

See if each report is needed. Assume, to begin, that all the reports have been wiped out and you must justify reinstating each one. What are the objectives of each report? What would be the consequences if each one were discontinued?

If you're in doubt about the value of a report, delay distributing it and see how many of those who usually receive it ask about it. If only a few ask, and the information is available elsewhere, eliminate the report.

Look for opportunities to consolidate reports to give more information in fewer pages.

Shorten Reports

Now that you've eliminated the unnecessary reports, shorten the ones you must produce. A chart or graph will often be worth many pages of narrative, and convey the information more sharply. Look at the writing. Is it simple and to the point? Is it clear and sharp?

Think of your readers. Are you telling them what they need to know? Above all, fight the tendency to tell them more than they need to know, or to tell them things they really don't need to know.

Target Unnecessary Paperwork

You can't eliminate all paperwork, says Dianna Booher in *Cutting Paperwork in the Corporate Culture,* but there are items that are excellent targets for reduction. Here are some of them:

- Customer cover letters that say only, "I'm sending you something; you have it in your hands now."
- Memos written as self-protection.
- Forms that collect duplicate information.
- Reams of computer printouts of information that has to be interpreted before it's usable.
- Reports that are requested but never read.
- Routine activity and trip reports.
- Distribution lists that include everyone who's anybody with any possibility of being needed in the next ten years.
- Fifty-page documents sent to a manager who wants only a page of conclusions and recommendations.
- Policy and procedure manuals that outline responses to every contingency possible.

If Not Needed

Here are some ways to eliminate reports once you've found they are unnecessary.

Start by stretching the report period. If it's a weekly report, try two weeks. If monthly, make it quarterly.

Cut its length. Get it to an overview message, recommendations, and a few details — or even shorter. If any readers want more details, let them ask for them.

Try attaching a cover memo to your report. Say, "To cut distribution costs and to reduce your reading load, I plan to stop sending this report unless I hear from you."

If you don't hear, stop sending it. You may find that no one wants the report. And if they ask for it, ask why they need it. You may find another report being issued will meet their needs.

If they still feel they need it, ask more questions. Is it timely? Could it be shorter, with fewer details? You may be able to at least shorten it, and thus better meet your readers' needs.

Use the MADE Format

If, as you should, you're writing to express rather than to impress, here's a system that will help you to give your readers information as quickly as possible.

Call it MADE. Try expressing yourself in this sequence:

M. Message. What is the bottom-line message of interest to your reader? ("The auditors have noted that some oil storage tank valves are not being locked.")

A. Action. What action do you plan to take, or expect the reader to take, based on the message? ("Please check in your region, and by August 15 give me a list of deficient sites and your plans for securing those sites.")

D. Details. Who, when, where, why, how, how much? Include only those details that are essential, usually the why and how. Often all necessary details are in the first paragraph. If so, don't add unnecessary ones.

E. Optional Evidence. Mention any attachments or enclosures you're sending to make the message clearer or the action easier to take. ("Enclosed is the company's latest lease security policy.")

Management Style

Management style — how you handle your staff and do your work — enters into the production of unnecessary reports.

Some managers document. They don't want to be held accountable, so they demand volumes of paperwork to prove they aren't responsible if things go wrong.

Others delay, distributing paper up the corporate ladder and laterally, hoping someone else will make a decision.

And still others delegate, sending paperwork downward, over and over, asking for more and more information. Everyone is kept busy, and all think the reports they are doing are causing the delay in reaching a decision.

Check Yourself

To make certain you aren't adding to the paper glut, ask yourself some questions.

Are people on your staff writing memos on phone conversations, rewriting policy, writing detailed activity reports on routine duties, or designing new forms to use? If your answer is yes, maybe you're overstaffed. And if you are, say so.

When things go wrong, do you ask what is the cause and how you can fix it? Or do you ask who is to blame? If the latter, expect a lot of "cover" memos and reports. Your employees see the need for self-protection. If you will concentrate on fixing the difficulty rather than the blame, that defensive paperwork will stop.

Do you really need those weekly reports, or is the information available in another report? Eliminate as many of them as you can. Ask your employees for "exception" reporting. Encourage them to bring to your attention things about which they need guidance, or to which you should be alerted.

When you compliment employees, don't base your compliments solely on paperwork such as sales records. To do this is to invite more and longer reports. Instead, compliment them for such things as good handling of angry customers, building goodwill with a client, or grooming a subordinate for promotion.

Do you ignore talk? If you do, people around you may learn that the way to get a response from you is to hand in a report. And up goes the paperwork.

When you start to write, ask why you're writing. And stop if you don't like the answer.

When your subordinates send you something worthless in writing, ask why. It will make them think twice about sending you more meaningless pages.

Finally, ask your boss why you're being asked to submit a report. If the report is necessary, the reply will help you to make it more useful. If the boss can't tell you why, you probably don't need to write it.

Hold That Blue Pencil

Many managers believe they haven't done their job unless they make a few changes in a letter or report prepared by subordinates. If this is a habit, and it contributes nothing to the writing, subordinates quickly learn this. The brighter among them will insert obvious errors, so the manager will have something to change, and thus be satisfied.

In business writing, there's a difference between editing and rewriting. Editing involves marking unclear or incorrect phraseology, then returning the work to the author. Rewriting means a complete overhaul. Careful on that. You'll get poor copy because "the boss always rewrites everything anyway."

Here are some areas of editing where you have to make decisions:

- Content. Raise questions about incorrect details and facts.
- Organization. If material isn't presented logically, go for a revision.
- Clarity. If writing is muddy or questions are left unanswered, call for some rewriting.
- Grammar and punctuation. Walk a middle line. Edit for any errors that reflect poorly on the company. Minor ones (a comma or not) may be style matters and not worth the cost involved in the rewriting or retyping.

Try to limit the number of people who have the power to change a document. One company traced a four-paragraph letter through seventeen rewrites before it went out.

Unnecessary Reports

Here are two findings that you should know about reports:

1. Many people label the reports they receive as unnecessary, but only 20 percent would put the reports they write in that class.
2. The higher up the officials, the more apt they are to think they both write and receive unnecessary reports.

Conclusion: the job of eliminating unnecessary reports falls to senior managers.

Chapter 13

Communicating

To move ahead, you must be able to communicate effectively with bosses, peers, subordinates, and customers. That means not only expressing yourself clearly, but tailoring your message to the needs, concerns, temperament, and even the vocabulary of your listeners.

One-on-one communications call for somewhat different strategies and skills than presentations or speeches. But if you start with the individual, you'll find it's easier to translate your skills to group communication situations.

Try for Rapport

Before you can communicate anything effectively to another person, you need a sense of rapport, says Genie Z. Laborde in *Influencing with Integrity*.

Rapport, the business of building a sense of faith or trust in the other party, is the most important part of any interaction.

You build rapport by finding common ground with the other person. You can also develop it subtly by matching the other person's voice or tempo, breathing rate, movements or gestures, or body postures.

What's Your Goal?

Before trying to communicate, you must determine what you're trying to accomplish. To identify and achieve your desired outcome, Laborde suggests this approach:

1. Aim for a specific result. Pinpoint exactly what you want the other party to comprehend.

2. Be positive. Communicate enthusiasm to the listener.

3. See, hear, and feel sensory data. Listen to the type of words others use and tailor your images accordingly. Some people relate to visual images such as "I hope to see my name in lights." Others are more auditory: "I loved it when the crowd started to cheer." Another possibility is touching or feeling sensations: "It was like walking on air."

4. Dovetail your desires with the listener's. View the other person as an ally, and try to achieve something for both of you.

5. Entertain short- and long-range objectives, communicating in a way that will help you to reach both.

What's a Good Communicator?

The essence of communication is people talking with people, observe Richard S. Ruch and Ronald Goodman in *Image at the Top*. Good communicators have an attitude of caring instantly, and it's sensed instantly by others. They can project and practice ideal communications. They refuse to become isolated from constituencies and have the ability to stand up to interrogations by telling the truth.

Effective corporate communications have to be based on honesty, the authors say. Try following these simple rules:

- **Tell it straight from the shoulder.** Plain talk, maybe salty and definitely colorful, make you and your communications real. Talk across to your audience, never down. Watch for hip-shooting and foot-in-mouth disease.
- **Be human.** And admit it. No one, no business is perfect. If you foul up, tell your constituencies. No one expects you to be superman. If your company is forced to retrench, tell them why and how.
- **Keep it simple.** Avoid jargon. Nothing is as potent as a polished, bare bones, well-presented idea.
- **Look for the drama.** Dig it out. Mix it with your communications. Let excitement in your business come through. You may find it fun.
- **Be a good listener.** Nose to the grindstone and ear to the ground. Get out and talk to your customers and employees.
- **Package your message attractively.** An interesting bottom line can be dull in plain black and white.
- **Keep it short.** Sift through it all and only present the nuggets of gold. Keep your eyes on what's important to the audience, not what's important to you.
- **Avoid legalese.** Don't sell out to the lawyers.
- **Saying won't make it so.** Trust in advertising will sell a lot more than shrill hyperbole.

Get Feedback

Fred Pryor, author of *The Energetic Manager,* would add a rule to this list:
- **Get feedback.** After you've talked with a person, make certain he or she understands what you're saying. This calls for getting feedback. "I want to know what you think about all this" is a way to seek such feedback. Then, if it is evident that persons don't understand what you're saying, you must clarify and refine your message.

This is time-consuming, of course. But not half as time-consuming as dealing with the problems that result from a lack of clear communications.

Verbal Persuasion

The authors of *Back-to-Basics Management* emphasize that before you can persuade, you must motivate the other person or persons to listen. To do that, respond to emotions with encouragement, reassurance, and praise. Encourage expression and tension release. You will have a more comfortable situation.

When Things Go Wrong

Things do go wrong, and when they do, managers indicate how skilled they are in managing, says Pryor.

Here are a few pointers for communicating when problems arise:

- Attack issues, not people.
- Ask for input and insight to solve problems.
- Avoid using labels such as "slow" or "incompetent."
- Give feedback that is pointed and specific. A report given you isn't "lousy." Instead, it may require further development in the section on possible solutions.

If you're meeting over a problem, use this four-step method of changing grips to goals, using it to ask for help rather than attacking others:

a. My frustration is_____

b. What I would like is_____

c. Therefore, my goal is_____

d. So the meeting subject is_____

Reading Body Language

Realize that your body language mirrors your verbal language.

Don't just read body language and interpret symbols at the unconscious level. Assign meanings at a conscious level, too. Work to understand the silent language of body gestures, eye motions, skin/touch sensations, and space (standing or sitting far apart).

Many gestures have more than one meaning. You must consider where it's done, who is present, and what preceded and followed the action. Remember that body language reflects feelings, not facts.

Here are some common body language signs and their possible meanings:

- Crossing arms or legs indicates defense.
- Lack of movement indicates that a person is trying not to be noticed, or is listening and planning, or is playing it safe.
- Leaning forward vs. sitting back is the difference between "tell me more, I'm interested" and "let me think about it; I may not be that interested."
- Cocking the head signals interest and a willingness to hear the opinions of others.
- Hands folded in the lap or on the stomach is a protective gesture.
- Hands placed on a desk says, "Let's get right down to business."

Chapter 14

You're on Stage

No matter how good your skills and virtues are, they won't advance your career unless others are aware of them.

You can't depend on your accomplishments to sell you. You must learn to sell yourself.

It's not as bad as it sounds. Selling yourself is simply a combination of trying to make a good impression on others and looking for and making the most of opportunities to let others know about what you've done and what you can do.

As Raymond C. Johnson puts it in *The Achievers,* you have to get your foot in the right doors and make a favorable impression on those who can help you toward success. And you can't get ahead if you don't feel confident and secure in your appearance and ability to express yourself.

Play the Role

You are on stage when you're at work, he said.

An actor projects a constant image of ability and confidence. If you want to be recognized as an outstanding manager or department head, be prepared to play the role at all times and back it up with extensive homework. Those you work with and for are your audience.

Acting, in this sense, includes looking the role you've chosen to play. Fine quality clothing and careful grooming are important to making your mark as an achiever. When you think you can't afford expensive clothing, buy them anyway. Often your dress is the first impression formed of you. Dress for your way of life and invest in your future.

Look the Part

When you're on that work stage, carry yourself like a supremely confident actor making an opening night entrance to thunderous applause. And stay in the character you've written for yourself.

The next step is a personal public relations program that allows others — friends, colleagues, neighbors — to sing your praises. People love to talk about important friends. Your success builds their importance.

Be subtle. Look for the right occasions to brag a bit, then give a copy of a newspaper clipping or other explanation of your achievement to others. They'll pass the word along.

Help Others

Other suggestions in *The Achievers* for becoming favorably known include:

- Help others to attain their goals. Sooner or later, they'll send opportunities your way.
- Analyze your habits and make a conscious effort to build on the good and eliminate the bad.
- Be enthusiastic. No quality attracts people more.
- Act enthusiastic. Most of the power of enthusiasm comes from its effect on others.
- Cultivate empathy. Try to put yourself in other people's shoes.
- Make friends. No one gets ahead alone.
- Ask for help. You gain the benefit of others' experience and expertise and most people like to be asked.

Planned Self-marketing

In *Blow Your Own Horn,* Jeffrey R. Davidson notes that self-marketing doesn't mean using people or employing deceit or trickery. It's not being boastful, arrogant, pushy, or egotistical.

The most effective self-marketing is done with class and honesty, based on a genuine respect and concern for the needs of others. The secret is to develop the skills that will make you a valuable professional and then to learn to promote those skills in a way that will earn you the respect and success you deserve.

Start by developing a plan. Define what you have to offer or want to offer the world. Draw up a career list of the things you want and don't want in your career. Focus on a few challenging, realistic goals. List the components of your ideal career or work situation, and consider these very specific goals. Finally, establish timetables for achieving those goals.

Become Indispensable

An effective marketer creates a niche for the product or service being promoted. To advance your career, you must create a niche for yourself. That means making yourself indispensable — the person supervisors ask for first when reorganizations begin, the office expert in certain subjects, the mentor to many junior employees. You can do this by finding out what is needed on the job, not just what is expected.

There are many ways to make yourself indispensable. Here are nine of them:

1. Take the unwanted job. Pick up a skill or technology that is vital to your company, but relatively hard to learn. Or be the best at something no one else wants to do.

2. Go the extra mile. Take on more work than you're assigned. Volunteer to help on a project that is running over deadline. Help out on rush jobs. Help a fellow worker who is having problems.

3. Work harder when unsupervised. You know how it is. The boss goes on vacation and production drops. Employees drift into each other's offices, stretch lunch hours, and make more personal phone calls. Do the opposite. Work extra hard. Try to complete jobs assigned to you before the boss left. There is nothing a supervisor appreciates more after a trip than "Here's the job you wanted. It's done." The subtle yet deep-seated message you convey is long-lasting.

4. Get credit for the group. Those who make it to the top levels of management are able to motivate others to do their best and to work well together. Those above you know that when a group does well, it's at least partly because someone exhibited leadership. If you were managing the group, you've proven your ability to facilitate good work.

5. Make your boss look good. Both bosses and their supervisors appreciate this. The best way to make your boss look good is to handle your work efficiently and thoroughly. A fair boss will give you credit for this, increasing your chances of promotion. If your boss leans on you heavily without giving you credit, you'll still probably win the promotion. That boss understands your importance to him and won't want to take a new position without your assistance.

6. Handle key client development. Each time you interact with a client, you are planting the seeds of a personal and professional relationship. If you've done your job well, that relationship becomes one of the company's most important assets.

7. Become a mentor. No matter how young you are, you may be in a position to help junior members of your firm. This can be accomplished on an informal basis, and you can choose the amount of energy you're willing to commit. Helping junior members looks good to those above you, especially at performance review time.

8. Be aware of a supervisor's needs. If your boss has been extra supportive of you, tell him or her that you appreciate it. Remember to praise your boss to your co-workers and other supervisors. Be sure to be honest. A phony attempt can be detected immediately.

9. Know what's needed. This means knowing the basics — being on top of your job, your department's goals, and your company's objectives. This strategy calls for specific actions.

Protect Yourself

Knowing your job description and following it, or getting it amended if necessary, will protect you from misunderstandings and give you a good idea of the part you play in the organization. This is important to both your work satisfaction and your chance of promotion.

Be sure to learn and understand the goals of your department. They are important to guide action as well as to mark milestones. Knowing your group's goals will help you to set priorities for your own work and to make intelligent decisions about how jobs should be done.

Be aware of your company's objectives. They may be to expand sales, increase mergers, or solidify a market. Your organization's brochure, annual report, promotional literature, or employee handbook should have the objectives spelled out. It should unify and give meaning to all the department goals. Be aware that the objectives can change with differing economic and market conditions.

If you aren't receiving sufficient guidance, look at any problem in light of your company's objectives.

Keys to Promotion

You can anticipate organizational changes and carve your own niche in any new structure. Do this by being on the lookout for needs you can fill in any new organizational chart, and be qualified to fill that need.

Often that means becoming an expert. And often that means that a new job, and a new title, will be created for you, so that you can carry out that aspect of the company's functions.

If you have already developed such expertise, make your superiors aware of your special knowledge and how much people depend on you to provide that knowledge.

Another way to increase your chances of promotion is to turn that annual performance review into an opportunity for better things.

To do this, keep track of your performance for a year. Review your appointment book, your list of goals, and other materials. Then compare how you've done with what you set out to do.

Armed with this, you can take more control of the performance review sessions.

Spread the Word

Create opportunities for more people to know you and your accomplishments.

Join local professional and community organizations and attend their meetings. Try to attend at least two major professional conventions a year.

Become an active member of your groups. Choose organizations that genuinely interest you and be active on committees and task forces.

Prepare to do some public speaking. Develop a few topics to speak on, look for organizations that might be interested, and send them letters explaining your background and the topics about which you can speak.

Have your articles published. This establishes your credentials as an expert and gets favorable exposure for you and your company. Start with in-house publications, then try for professional and general newsletters or magazines. Submit suggestions before you write an article, focusing on successful work you've done. "How-to" formats are always popular.

Prepare reprints of your articles and circulate them to friends and associates.

Chapter 15

Skills for the Future

Career success is a moving target for the years ahead. Good organizational and communications skills are a must. So is keeping up with the latest trends in your field.

But what else will it take to keep moving up in your company in an era marked by constant change and hot individual and corporate competition?

Many experts have peered into their crystal balls trying to help ambitious men and women identify and develop the skills they'll need to get ahead.

In *Creating Excellence*, Craig R. Hickman and Michael A. Silva say the successful managers of the future will be those who master six interdependent "New Age" skills.

1. Creative insight: Asking the right questions. This requires concentration and adopting a variety of perspectives so you can ask questions from far-ranging points of view — questions others might not think of asking.

Insight forces you to move away from reliance on rules, logic, efficiency, and black and white thinking to get at the heart of a problem, not just its visible symptoms. Asking the right questions — and you have to ask a lot of questions — enables you to discover all facets of an issue, the hidden opportunities, advantages, and strengths, opening the door to the best strategies.

2. Sensitivity: Doing unto others. Understand people's moods and expectations, and act on that understanding. To bind people together so they feel motivated to achieve high goals, you have to look inside each individual to gain knowledge of that person's expectations and needs. All people are not the same, and they're certainly not all the same as you. People don't stay the same throughout their lives, either.

3. Vision: Creating the future. Vision is a mental journey from the known to the unknown, creating the future from a montage of facts, figures, hopes, dreams, dangers, and opportunities.

An offensive and a defensive skill, vision helps you to position yourself and your organization to create and take advantage of opportunities. You search out ideas and concepts that add up to a vision, articulate that vision, and persuade others to embrace it and look for ways to develop it.

Vision helps to chart a course that creates change and helps you to respond to external changes. It joins strategy and culture to achieve corporate excellence.

4. Versatility: Anticipating change. Welcome change as an opportunity, not a threat, and learn to control it to your advantage.

Change is unavoidable, and there's no point in resisting it.

Develop goals beyond your immediate problems and pursue interests outside your own field. That will keep you from getting too complacent or inflexible. Stay alert to anything in your environment that might signal a trend or change in customer or competitor behavior and move in a bold but orderly fashion to make those changes work for you.

5. Focus: Implementing change. To exploit change effectively, take a step-by-step approach. Assess how a particular change will affect your organization before you start. Be sure it's realistic for you. Determine what specific people and operational changes it will require. Still realistic? If so, develop a plan and timetable for shifting focus, then begin implementation, monitoring and adjusting as you go. And always be prepared for the inevitable surprises.

6. Patience: Living in the long term. Move away from the emphasis on short-term returns on investment and fast-track careers. You can have immediate goals, but you need a long-term view that evaluates those goals in terms of a more distant future.

Rise above the thoughts and actions of others and have the patience to see your vision through.

Patience helps you to use the other five "New Age" skills at the right time and in the right combination and proportion.

PART III

HOW TO GET THE MOST FROM OTHER PEOPLE

You don't operate in a vacuum. Other people play vital roles in your life and you can't succeed unless you can manage your relationships in a way that moves you toward your goals.

Of course, other people have goals, too. One of the keys to productive relationships is learning how to create situations that benefit all parties. A manager, after all, is defined as one who gets things done through other people. That requires sensitivity to their needs and wants as well as skill in creating a team that's pulling in the same direction.

This part of the book explores some of the critical interactions in business and offers specific approaches you can use to handle such potentially difficult tasks as hiring, firing, motivating, giving feedback, and delegating.

This part also covers negotiating — a subtle skill you need in a wide range of business and personal dealings.

You'll also find detailed suggestions on getting the most from the most common business interaction of all: meetings.

Finally, this part discusses leadership. You'll see how all the abilities and skills discussed in this book come together to develop leadership and make it work.

As you read this part, keep in mind the advice of Dale Carnegie, author of the timeless classic, *How to Win Friends and Influence People*.

Carnegie points out that people are not creatures of logic but of emotion. And the only way to get anyone to do anything is to make the other person want to do it. You influence other people by talking about what they want and showing them how to get it.

When you have a brilliant idea, let others cook and stir it themselves. They will then regard it as their own and like it better.

Other key Carnegie principles to remember as you finish reading this book:

- Become genuinely interested in other people.
- Make the other person feel important and do it sincerely.
- Try honestly to see things from the other person's point of view.
- Make the other person happy about doing what you suggest.

Chapter 16

Hire the Right People

You need all of your communicating, listening, decision-making, and "people" skills working in top form when you're hiring.

Interviewing and hiring new employees is, if done right, one of the most important ways to achieve your goals. With the right team in place, you can move ahead more quickly and effectively.

Many people neglect to give the interviewing and hiring processes the attention they deserve.

Robert Heller observes in *The Supermanagers* that picking the right people for the right jobs is a high-risk area. It can never be an exact science, but you can learn to go beyond your "gut feeling" to make productive choices.

Get the Facts

First, get the facts. Check out what you see on the résumé. Follow up every reference.

At the interview, notice whether the applicant is observant (looking around your office for indications of your interests). Do you feel that you are being listened to and understood? Do you get more than "yes" and "no" answers? Do you see signs of boredom or impatience? Is there free admission of mistakes or confessions of ignorance on some counts?

Remember that you're trying to hire. The purpose isn't not to hire. You're after proof that the person has the qualities and abilities you're looking for.

Two Rules for Hiring

Robert Townsend summarizes his hiring philosophy in *Further Up the Organization*.

To keep an organization young and fit, he says, don't hire anyone until everybody is overworked. That way your people will welcome the newcomer no matter who. Besides, a new person who comes aboard in circumstances other than absolutely necessary makes people wonder what's happening in the organization.

Rule one in hiring is to take your time. Tell the candidate who's pressing you to cool it or take the other offer. Get to know each candidate as well as you can. Remember, if you pick a lemon, you'll suffer.

Rule two in hiring, and it's particularly important when all of the candidates seem outstanding, is to hire the one for whom you would prefer to work.

Candidate Assessment

What makes for success in hiring? In *1000 Things You Never Learned in Business School,* William N. Yoemans states that good executives have learned to see a candidate clearly in terms of the two things that count — evidence that he or she can do the job at hand, plus the personality and character that's right for the organization.

Start by analyzing the job, in terms of the skills it calls for, the responsibilities it entails. Gauging each candidate accurately calls for some gut sensitivity and a lot of reading between the lines. One way to do this is to pick a subject to talk about that's neutral but not trivial, and try to establish a warm rapport.

Ask for Details

When it's time to turn to the nitty-gritty, don't hesitate to ask for details. Most résumés list past experience that lends itself to exploration. With the requirements of your own situation in mind, ask something like, "How would you tackle that problem today?" or "What would you have done if the test results were less promising?" What you're after here is quality of thinking. The more specific you get, the more you'll learn.

When you interview someone, be careful about leaping to first impressions. From time to time, try saying nothing and see what happens. In any case, do a lot of listening. It's important to find out what the candidate wants to ask. Are the questions frivolous and self-serving, or is there a professional level of interest in the job? People are anxious to know about such things as working hours. They do, after all, have personal lives. But there can be revealing nuances in all of this, if you know how to spot them.

If the interview leaves you definitely uninterested, you may find it more comfortable to talk around the bad news and handle it by letter. Courtesy suggests that you do this within two weeks.

The Hiring Process

Beverly A. Potter suggests certain interview principles in *Changing Performance on the Job.*

Establish rapport. Put candidates at ease with casual comments. Be relaxed but attentive.

Don't talk too much. When you're talking, you are not getting information about the candidate.

Maintain control. Decide what topics to cover and stay on target. Cut off irrelevant chatter.

Don't be interviewed. Acknowledge questions about the job and company, but hold them off until you want to discuss them. This will keep your interview on track.

Avoid leading questions. Don't suggest the desired answer with a question like "Are you looking for responsibility?" Of course the candidate will say yes. Don't give any clue as to what answer you want, with questions such as this one: "What are you looking for in a job?"

Don't jump to conclusions. Interviewers tend to interpret vague general statements like "I want a job with potential" according to their own expectations and stereotypes. Don't make assumptions.

Get specific information. Ask questions that will give you specifics about experience, skills, and work habits.

Effective Interviewing Techniques

Try these interviewing techniques to get more information quickly out of job candidates:

Be an active listener. That means giving verbal feedback like "uh huh" or "hmmm," or nonverbal responses like nodding and smiling that communicate interest.

Repeat. Repeat a key word or echo it with a slight inflection to get amplification of a general word or phrase.

Probe. Ask open-ended questions that begin with how, when, who, what, in what way, or which, to get a particular point clarified. Don't ask questions that bring only a yes or no response. Don't ask why. This implies justifying something and puts people on the defensive.

Silence. When a candidate is speaking relevantly and pauses or stops, remain silent for a moment. The candidate generally will continue on the subject.

Check answers. Probe to clarify and get specific information. If the candidate says, "It was a good job," ask, "Do you mean you liked the people you worked with?" Whether you are right or not, the candidate will clarify. Present your question tentatively to reduce defensiveness.

Sum up. When you reach the end of a section of your interview, summarize the candidate's main points, then ask, "Is there anything else?" This gives the candidate an opportunity to add more. If not, you can move on to the next topic.

Use this same method to end the interview, summarizing the main points discussed and asking if there is anything else. If you've forgotten or missed information important to the candidate, the person will repeat it. If you've misunderstood, the candidate will correct you. If the candidate forgot something, this is an opportunity to add it.

This technique of summing up can also be used to get a wandering interview back on target.

Demonstrate Skills

Some candidates can demonstrate skills. A sales person could deliver a product pitch. An editor could edit a sample text.

To evaluate administrative ability, try the in-basket approach. Assemble a packet of letters and memos. Provide a brief situation scenario, then have the candidate read over each item and write out an appropriate action and rationale. This lengthy exercise can be taken home by the candidate and done there.

Use role playing to assess complex interaction skills such as supervision. If you're interviewing electronic assembler trainees, for example, have the R&D department develop a task that requires eye-hand coordination and manual dexterity.

Look Within

To find the best employees for promotions, Lee Bowes, who wrote *No One Need Apply,* suggests a different tack.

Look within, she advises. Those people know the company, have proven abilities, and when promoted, can hit the ground running. Hiring costs will be minimal. In addition, promoting from within sends a loud voice throughout your company: Jobs aren't dead-end here. Thus the best and brightest won't be tempted to move elsewhere, and the turnover at the entry level will be reduced.

And to find new employees? Use networks. She bases this on two beliefs: 1. People are hired because they know somebody. 2. Hiring through networking is an effective way to get the best possible candidates. Here are some ways to do that:

● Establish employee networks, so employees know about job openings and can recommend their friends. Most employees will recommend only the best. They feel their own reputations are hanging on the recommendation. This approach will pay off by identifying people who can do the work and will stay with you.

This is particularly useful if you want more minorities in a department.

● Create new networks by attending job fairs and meetings of professional associations, where job-seekers abound.

Keep Interviews Short

Bowes believes lengthy interviews are a waste of time. But abbreviated ones can help you by allowing you to measure a candidate's sophistication, adaptability, and interpersonal skills. You can judge how well a candidate will fit into the corporate structure, recognizing that very competent people, stars in other firms, can perform miserably in your company simply because they don't fit in.

One reason for interviews is to make the candidate want to work for you. This means everyone meeting the candidate should sell the firm, or you'll miss out on some of the best people.

When filling new positions or vacancies, don't toss aside those unsolicited letters and resumes. These persons who have taken an interest in your firm can be excellent potential employees.

Dealing with Applicants

Here's a step-by-step system for handling the applicants for a position in your company:

1. Have all candidates fill out a standard application form, showing work history, dates of employment, and salary history. This is much more reliable than their own résumés.

2. Interview those who meet strict requirements. Spend ten to thirty minutes per candidate.

3. Schedule detailed interviews for those who pass these first two steps. You are now trying to assess which of several candidates is best. These interviews should take about an hour. Spend ten to fifteen minutes on the question, "Can you briefly say what your work and work history have been?"

Look for Advancement

Look for some progression in a career, some sign of commitment. Find out why the candidate left each key position.

Get as much background as you can on the most recent position the person held. Go into detail on responsibilities handled, supervisory experience, and job accomplishments.

Then describe a job or task and ask each applicant how he or she would approach it. Describe a problem you had and ask applicants what they would have done. Finally, discuss the salary histories and expectations of each applicant.

Chapter 17

Firing: It Must Be Done

Sometimes you'll make a mistake in hiring. Or you may inherit a person who can't or won't do the job. Then you'll be faced with the task most people dread most: firing an employee.

Firing someone is never pleasant, but there are ways to do it that minimize the pain for both of you.

A Test of Leadership

In his book *Managing,* former ITT head Harold Geneen calls firing a test of leadership for the company and the executive.

There is no formula for doing it, he notes, as he analyzes three typical situations.

If a person has done a poor job, and knows it, you are faced with a question: was it because he wasn't helped? He was entitled to that help, so perhaps it wasn't his fault, and it was you who failed.

Look for Reason

Sometimes a person fails because he inherited a tough problem that no one else could solve, or because he was caught in a situation completely beyond his control.

The most difficult of all is firing the person who works hard, doing the best he can, but whose confidence in himself far outstrips his abilities. He's in over his head. His judgment or lack of judgment might even endanger the whole operation.

It's difficult to tell such a person that he is incompetent. After all, you may have given him raises and promotions for years. It was you who put him in water over his head.

Finally, there's the person who has served the company faithfully for twenty or more years, and now is failing in health and ability. Perhaps he's a few years from retirement. What do you do with him?

Handling each of these cases will determine what kind of a leader you are.

Probably you will let the first two go, but keep the third. He has earned his right to stay on, even at the expense of efficiency. If possible, move him laterally and let someone else take over his job. If you fired him, the message would be clear: It's company policy to pay you as long as you're useful, and then throw you on the junk heap when you're old and gray. No one would give loyalty to a company like that.

Keep Records

The editors of *Working Woman* put it succinctly in the summary of *The Working Woman Report:*

If an employee is not doing well, keep records of unsatisfactory work, criticisms, and warnings. Try to help him or her to reform by discussing specific problems and possible improvements.

If you must fire someone, don't wait. Do it in your office, with the door closed. Make certain it's not a holiday or the person's birthday. Don't dwell on your affection for the person, stress your guilt or discomfort, or act too brisk or coldly businesslike. At the other extreme, don't hold out false hopes that the person will be hired again, don't allow the employee to stay on indefinitely, and be thorough in describing the company's termination policy.

We hope you know this already: don't discuss with others your reasons for the firing.

Legal Aspects

Firing an employee may have many legal ramifications. So be sure you follow your company's procedures to the letter, checking with the personnel department every step of the way. If you have to perform this unpleasant task, you want to be sure it will stick.

Chapter 18

Motivation: It's Up to You

Even the best people won't perform up to their capabilities without a motivating environment — and a manager with leadership skills.

One Motivation Strategy

Former football great Fran Tarkenton offers a comprehensive motivation system in *How to Motivate People*.

People don't change their behavior unless it makes a difference to them to do so, he says. You have to recognize that you can't change a person's mental state or some cause of their behavior. What you can change is the external behavior, and you can change that by manipulating the consequences.

That's as much a matter of rewarding good behavior as it is of changing poor behavior. Provide positive reinforcement for "normal" behavior as well as for superior work.

Tarkenton says that most workers do a good job about 80 percent of the time. If they do poor work more frequently than that, they don't last long.

Managers focus on the 20 percent of the time when workers are performing under par and allow the time that they work well to go by unnoticed. The individual concludes that if he doesn't foul up, nobody is going to notice he's there. He may even be encouraged to perform badly because that at least will get him noticed.

Rules of Behavior

Tarkenton offers these three rules of behavior for you to remember:

1. Good behavior that is reinforced by positive consequences tends to continue or to improve. (A plant supervisor creates a new preventive maintenance system. His boss writes him a letter of appreciation. From that day onward, that system will be checked and updated.)

2. Behavior that is demotivated by negative consequences tends to decrease. (The boss criticizes the plant manager for not having a preventive maintenance system. The plant supervisor will look into that deficiency in the near future.)

3. Good, productive behavior that goes unnoticed tends to decrease over time. (The plant manager's herculean effort is seen by top managers as "just part of his job description." Expect Hercules to turn into Tom Thumb. Nobody will continue to perform well unless you reinforce his motivation to do so.)

One of the American business community's principal challenges is to overcome the traditional managerial view that "you don't reward somebody for doing what he's supposed to do." We must move toward a policy of expending as much energy in keeping the up side up as keeping the down side down.

The Right Rewards

Financial rewards are only one motivating factor, and never the most important one. If they were, GM workers would be outperforming Toyota workers three to one.

Tarkenton says he knows this sounds corny, but equally important to getting people moving are such things as a letter of appreciation, coffee and doughnuts when they don't expect them, the human touches that make a job worth doing. And this is particularly true when the person you're trying to motivate is a sales rep or a secretary — not a superstar.

It's these people managers prefer to ignore. Managers have time to tack up an "Employee of the Week" award or punish a worker whose sloppiness costs the company down time, but ignore the large number of people in between, not eagles or slackers, who may need reinforcement more than that Employee of the Week or that slacker.

The PRICE System

Tarkenton applies behavioral principles through what he calls the PRICE Motivation System. That acronym stands for Pinpointing, Recording, Involvement, Consequences, and Evaluation.

Pinpoint the behavior you are trying to influence, then set precise objectives of what needs to be done, by whom, and by what date. Objectives must be realistic, easily understood, meaningful, and the result of every member of the team getting together to set them.

Recording, keeping score, is a motivator in business as it is in sports. Keep score of performance: production scores, weekly waste retrieval results, any other performances that can be measured. And post those scores publicly. Then tie results to positive consequences such as bonuses and promotions.

Scorekeeping lets each individual and group know how they're doing and how their performance ties in with the organization's. In addition to any tangible consequences such as bonuses, people gain the satisfaction of knowing they have contributed to a winning team.

Involvement means getting away from the old boss vs. worker mindset and getting people to play a real role in their work. It takes a while for a participative approach to get off the ground, but it does work and the benefits of getting the most from everyone extend to individuals and the company.

Consequences are where you actually start to change behavior. You can provide positive reinforcement, negative reinforcement, or no reinforcement.

The last is the most typical and the most useless. Poor behavior doesn't change and positive behavior that goes unnoticed may change for the worst.

Tie consequences directly to performance improvement. When someone does something right, let them know immediately that you've noticed and appreciate it. When you want to change the behavior, proceed just as quickly. Focus on the behavior and not the person, and make it clear that change is a must.

Evaluation, the last stage in the process is determining whether what you tried worked. Did you pinpoint the behaviors that were holding you back? Were you on target with recording, involvement, and consequences? Keep fine-tuning the system.

Remember — in the end the most successful managers will be those who can motivate to win because they understand what turns people on.

The Motivation Climate

In *1000 Things You Never Learned in Business School,* William N. Yoemans says creating a climate that motivates is an important part of a business leader's job.

People in such a climate radiate self-respect. They always know what's going on in their organization, what's expected of them, and how they're doing. They never feel isolated because both their achievements and their problems are acknowledged continually. At even the lowest level, each has some kind of start-to-finish responsibility that keeps him from feeling like a cog in some vast, impersonal machine.

Not an Accident

This kind of thing doesn't happen accidentally. As a manager, you should do all you can to create a climate in which all feel involved at all times, and are expected to make most of their own decisions. What you offer is the clear outlines of a goal. You're there to advise and help.

Your people should know that they can explore new and offbeat approaches, even take judicious risks, without fear of forfeiting your support. They should also know that they'll be called in next week to hear how much sales rose (or fell) as a result of their most recent efforts. A manager's role as intelligent coach, informant, and cheerleader mustn't be underestimated.

Another aspect of motivating is providing access to the boss. People need to know that they can come to you with problems and get a respectful and constructive response. The subject may seem unimportant to you, but to the other guy it's anything but. When they ask for help, give it to them, or explain why you can't. Don't leave anyone hanging, unless you're willing to accept a sudden but subtle transfer of responsibility. Of course, if this is an area in which you feel they should be making their own decisions, say so.

The Power in Your Hands

As manager, you have the power to raise or lower subordinates' levels of motivation, John Adair says in *Effective Leadership*.

Human motives have their sources in the deeper needs and values within people. A need that becomes conscious is called a want. A leader can help the process by which needs are transformed into wants. As leader, you can also work with each individual to realize those wants in the context of the common task.

Five Musts of Motivation

If you are to influence for the common good, if you are to address personal wants, you'll need an understanding of motivational chemistry. For motivation and job satisfaction to be strong, rather than adequate or weak, each individual must:

1. Feel a sense of personal achievement in the job he is doing, and must believe that he is making a worthwhile contribution to the objectives of the group or section.

2. Feel that the job itself is challenging, is demanding the best of the individual, is giving him the responsibility to match his capabilities.

3. Receive adequate recognition for his achievements.

4. Have control over those aspects of his job which have been delegated to him.

5. Feel that he, as an individual, is developing, that he is advancing in experience and ability.

To provide the right climate and opportunities for these five musts to be met for each individual in the group is possibly the most difficult, the most challenging and rewarding of the leader's tasks.

Specific Motivators

What about specific motivators? The key, says Henry C. Rogers in *The One-Hat Solution,* is to find the trigger that will encourage people to do better.

Some believe only money will do it. Money is important up to a point, but in most cases it's just a way to keep score. It indicates that people are appreciated, too, that they enjoy a certain position in the company. The actual dollars constitute only a small part of the motivation. Titles are the same. Everyone wants a title because it indicates a rise above the rest.

Hand Out Praise

Make a point of praising anyone who does a job "above and beyond the call of duty." This might include working overtime to get the job completed, working on a weekend, solving a problem that has perplexed everyone, or handling an assignment that wins the approval of a client. Try giving praise, too, to those who are doing a routinely good job. They'll try even harder.

By praising people, you make them feel important. Now they're ready to extend themselves, and there's a good chance their levels of performance will skyrocket.

Praise the Sales Force

In *Thriving on Chaos,* Tom Peters emphasizes that to be successful, a firm must be as close as possible to its consumers. The people in most companies who have this role are the sales and service forces. They are the firm to most customers. If your company and our American industry are to become competitive, those people close to the consumer must achieve preeminence.

Overinvest in dollars and people for your front lines sales, service, and distribution people and those who support them, Peters says. Pay them well. Train them excessively. Give them the tools and the opportunity to participate. Listen to them. Above all, praise them. Make them the company heroes. Companies who do this find their "ordinary" people do extraordinary things.

How Do You Rate on Motivating?

Take this test — but the rating of your answers is up to you. One piece of advice on it: Work on any negative responses.

	Yes	No
Have you agreed with each of your subordinates about main targets and continuing responsibilities, together with standards of performance, so that you both can recognize achievement?		
Do you recognize the contribution of each member of the group and encourage other team members to do the same?		
In the event of success, do you acknowledge it and build on it? In the event of setbacks, do you identify what went well and give constructive guidance for improving future performance?		
Can you delegate more? Can you give more discretion over decisions and more accountability to a sub-group or individual?		
Do you show to those that work with you that you trust them?		
Are there adequate opportunities for training and (where necessary) retraining?		
Do you encourage each individual to develop his capacities to the fullest?		
Is the overall performance of each individual regularly reviewed in face-to-face discussion?		
Does financial reward match contributions?		
Do you make sufficient time to talk and listen, so that you understand the unique and changing profile of needs and wants in each person, so that you can work with the grain of nature rather than against it?		
Do you encourage able people with the prospect of promotion within the organization, or, if that is impossible, counsel them to look elsewhere for the next position fitting their merit?		

Chapter 19

Give Valuable Feedback

As the motivational approaches make clear, it's extremely important for people to know where they stand. You have to provide continuous feedback, and it has to be feedback that's specific and directed to both the situation at hand and the goals you as manager and the employee are trying to reach.

Good feedback must be built on clear goals and checkpoints so that the person knows what to do or not to do and what specific behavior you're commenting on.

Most people have trouble giving feedback properly, notes Patricia King in *Performance Planning and Appraisal*.

Both praise and criticism are difficult for managers to handle. Many managers praise too seldom. Some never do. Yet praising the behavior you want to see continued can be one of your most powerful management tools.

Avoid sounding insincere by looking for specific behaviors to praise. People often interpret vague praise as phony, and nothing more than manipulative flattery. Even if your employees have a hard time accepting a compliment, they will hear it and it will have its effect if it's sincere.

Offering Criticism

You may avoid criticizing your subordinates because you fear their reactions. Or you may need to get angry in order to voice your criticism. Either of these behaviors robs you of the chance to influence your employees positively.

Deliver criticism in a matter-of-fact manner with little or no emotion. Focus only on the behavior and the work problem it causes. Be ready to handle the defensive reaction you're likely to get. Do this by assuring the employee that you know that no harm was meant.

Finally, express your faith that together you can solve the problem. You may need to describe again the behavior and the work problem it causes. Offer your help and support, but make it clear that you expect the subordinate to cooperate by taking responsibility for solving the problem.

Your subordinate may have personal problems that affect job performance. Be careful to concentrate only on how the problems affect the job. Beyond that, turn to professionals in your organization for advice, and encourage the person to seek help either within or outside the organization.

Don't assess character. Concentrate instead on what the subordinate did or didn't do, and why objectives were or were not met.

Guidelines

Here are guidelines for managers offering praise or criticism:

When praising: Do it often. Be specific and be direct.

When criticizing: Make it specific. Suggest what to do. Offer encouragement by expressing your faith that the person can change. Offer your own help.

Rewards

Give some thoughts to developing various ways to reward people for doing the right thing. A reward is nothing more than a manager paying attention to a worker, according to Marvin Karlins, author of *The Human Use of Human Resources.*

Your goal should be to give each worker the reward that best satisfies that worker's needs. You'll usually have to vary rewards so that boredom doesn't set in. There are many from which to choose:

- Praise, when honestly deserved, works well if you use it equally for similar performance, but not so frequently that it loses effectiveness.
- Public recognition for outstanding services rendered to the company is often highly appreciated.
- Job security is an effective reward, particularly in layoff-prone industries and for older workers.
- Money is a satisfying reward for everyone.
- Fringe benefits are effective in some cases, but most companies have a sufficiently strong benefits package to limit the value of this reward.
- Employee development programs that allow the individual to build job, leadership, or personal skills help keep workers sharp. Be sure the individual actually wants job enrichment and isn't being overwhelmed with new responsibilities.
- Involvement in decision-making gives employees a feeling of having some say in their own destinies and the operation of the company. It also enhances employees' understanding of the company's general workings and problems.
- More leisure time, by telescoping either production or work time, can be an effective motivator that also creates savings for the employer.

A four-day week, with ten-hour workdays, gives workers more free time and often enhances their motivation on the job.

- Opportunity for achievement and advancement in the organization is an important reward for capable employees.
- Greater freedom at work is also a valuable reward for the best employees, who often perform better when not closely watched by management.
- Finally, feedback itself is a reward. People want to know. Be informational and nonjudgmental, corrective but not critical when there's something you want to change.

Chapter 20

Improve Your Delegating Skills

Never do anything that someone else can do for you, as well or better. That's the advice of Raymond C. Johnson, author of *The Achievers*.

Simply put, delegation begins by determining all the tasks that must be performed to reach your organization's goals. Then select the individual or individuals best qualified to handle each duty and empower them to do it. Finally, check results regularly to make sure the productivity goals you've set are being reached or surpassed.

Why People Don't Delegate

In *Delegation*, Robert B. Nelson says these are the excuses managers give for not delegating:

1. My employees lack the experience.

2. It takes more time to explain than to do the job myself.

3. A mistake by an employee could be costly.

4. My position enables me to get quicker action.

5. There are some things that I shouldn't delegate to anyone.

6. My employees are specialists, and they lack the overall knowledge that many decisions require.

7. My people are already too busy.

8. My employees just aren't ready to accept more responsibility.

9. I'm concerned about lack of control over employee performance when I delegate.

10. I like keeping busy and making my own decisions.

11. Delegating is terrifying to me.

Insecurity?

Johnson says that the most common reason for failure to delegate is deep-seated insecurity. This self-defeating attitude influences how you accept and recognize the performance of those who work under you.

If this is your problem, ask yourself these questions: Is my assistant really after my job? Am I afraid he will do the work better than I can? Am I afraid to give him either overt praise or more authority because I fear he will replace me?

If this is your attitude, it's holding you back. Failing to share authority and responsibility may protect your immediate status at the expense of an opportunity to move up. The fastest way to promotion is to have a solid understudy in the wings, ready and able to step into your shoes when the time comes.

Finally, delegating some of your authority only makes your work easier.

Remember Your Benefits

When you delegate, don't think of it as doing the other person a favor. The use of effective delegation, says Robert Nelson, will pay off for you, as manager, and your company in many ways.

You will mobilize resources to achieve more results than you ever thought possible. You will have more time for managerial activities. These are the jobs — project planning, monitoring team members, and handling personnel problems — that no one else can do. You will focus on doing a few tasks very well, rather than doing a lot rather poorly.

You will increase your managerial potential. You will have someone trained to succeed you, so you will not be shackled to one particular area.

The organization benefits in many ways. Output goes up, work is completed more efficiently, and employees feel free to offer new ideas and suggestions to improve the operation of the company. Decision-making is improved, so the organization becomes more responsive and thus more competitive in the marketplace.

The Delegating Procedure

There's more to delegating than saying, "Do what I tell you to do," cautions Stephanie Winston in *The Organized Executive*.

It's entrusting the matter to the other person. It involves mutual commitment. The person to whom you are delegating makes a commitment to meet your expectations. For you, it means a commitment to give staff full cooperation, backing, and recognition.

Four-Point Procedure

A four-point procedure is involved in effective delegation.

1. Define the purpose and importance of the project, together with its deadline and the scope of the delegatee's responsibility.

The responsibility for clarification lies with you. Don't expect your employees to ask enough questions to clarify this.

If possible, get your employees to set their own deadlines. They're more apt to meet those.

Try to delegate a whole job, not bits and pieces. Staffers can waste a lot of time trying to put the pieces together to make a whole job. They also feel a greater sense of responsibility when handling an entire job.

2. Provide the necessary authority, resources, and support.

Make sure your subordinate has the authority needed to complete the task. Otherwise, the staffer's requests to others for help and information may be ignored because they don't come from you. It's up to you to clarify the staffer's degree of authority and autonomy.

3. Delegate for results. The key here is accountability, setting standards and making sure staffers know they're responsible for meeting those standards. For example, don't rewrite poor work. Return it with comments and the demand for a better job.

But be careful here. It's important not to confuse tactics with goals. Set a standard for results, but don't hamstring your staff by overcontrolling how they do their work.

When a problem arises, don't second-guess your staffer by making a decision over his head. Use the opportunity to show him or her how to handle it.

4. Review progress and follow-up. Setting deadlines and enforcing them establish a company tempo, ensuring that decisions are made promptly and tasks are handled with dispatch.

For ordinary purposes, follow up with calendar or tickler files. But if the job assignments are very complex or numerous, you may need to set up an assignment control log. This records all department projects. It shows dates, nature of assignment, to whom assigned, dates due, any postponements, and completion dates. This log is a ready source of data for performance evaluations, and ensures that staffers receive credit for their work.

Slowly Reduce Supervision

In *Work Smart, Not Hard,* George Sullivan offers advice about delegating.

On a first assignment, he writes, give the person as much supervision as you feel is required. Reduce it on the second assignment if the person was quick and efficient in completing the first task. This will save you time and increase the abilities of the person handling the task.

Encourage all who work for you to increase their duties and responsibilities. For example, a secretary who is a whiz at typing should be encouraged to try writing the letters as well.

Watch Out!

Once you've assigned a task, don't be manipulated into relieving the subordinate of the responsibility for taking the next step.

Here's how that can work: John meets you in the hallway and says, "Boss, we've got a problem . . ."

Say the wrong thing, such as "Let me get back to you in an hour," and John has put the weight back on your shouldlers.

Instead, see to it that the next move is his. "You're right. There is a problem. Give me a call tomorrow and tell me how it should be handled."

Selecting the Right Persons

One of the most crucial steps is selecting the right persons for jobs. You have to consider factors such as these:

● **Friction.** Disagreement between you and the person taking the assignment is healthy while the assignment is being made. It's only a problem if it extends into the execution stage.

● **Track record.** Match the job to the person. Past performance is significant only as it relates to the job you are delegating.

● **Location.** Don't delegate just because someone is close by and convenient to use, or maybe just not busy. Suit the job to the person.

● **Organization level.** If you want to delegate a job to someone several levels down in the organization, first confer with his or her supervisors and explain the situation. It will make the delegation smoother and keep noses from getting out of joint.

● **Compatibility.** Ideally, the styles of both persons involved are complementary. You're not looking for a carbon copy of yourself. You're looking for someone who can do the job.

Robert Nelson says you should consider four factors when selecting a person for an assignment. You should know each person's record for success on similar assignments, and how well they work with others. You should know their interests in such assignments. You need to know the professional interests and goals of each employee. Finally, you must consider which employees have the time to take on the task. Remember, when considering this, that some people work best handling routine assignments every day, while others, realizing they can advance only through work and achievement, are far more interested in receiving assignments.

Getting Their Trust

To get delegating to work, the persons to whom you delegate must have trust in you.

Talk isn't enough to create this. You must back up the employee who needs support sometimes even though you may not agree with a decision that's been made.

Don't harp on errors. Those making them usually know it. Instead, give them a chance to correct them.

Be open with your people. Don't try to hide your errors. Provide any information about the organization that would be helpful.

As you're working with your team members, clarify their expectations so they know in advance what is expected of them. Treat them with courtesy and respect.

Giving Assignments

As a manager, one of your most important jobs is communicating while delegating. Effective delegation demands effective communication. Without it, assignments are blurred, deadlines are vague, and results are predictably poor.

Communicating calls for mutual consultation and agreement between the manager and team members. It calls, too, for you to solicit team members' reactions and ideas throughout the process.

Start by telling team members very clearly what they are being asked to do. Describe the performance standards to be used to evaluate the work, and make sure the team has, and knows it has, both the authority to do the job and the level of support (money and other resources) required.

Evoke a feeling of obligation and commitment within team members, then establish a system to reward outstanding performances.

During this communicating process, focus on results rather than ways to accomplish the task. That way, team members will learn more, take more initiative, and have greater enthusiasm for the task.

Evaluating

As a follow-up to any assignment, you should appraise the completed task and discuss your evaluation with the team member. Measure the degree of success against the standards set when you made the assignment. This should provide insight for both of you, showing how each performed, as well as suggesting how you worked together as a team.

At this time, ask yourself two questions: Was the task completed as intended in a timely manner? What could be done to delegate such a task better in the future?

Failure usually is due to a lack of understanding about what was to be done or to a lack of authority for completing the task. If either of these caused less-than-expected results, you need to pay attention to communication when delegating a task. You must clearly describe the task, then ask the team member or members to speak up if the delegated authority turns out to be inadequate.

Discuss your evaluation of their work with team members. This should be a two-way exchange of perceptions and feedback on each other's work style.

You should provide both positive and negative comments so team members will understand what they are doing well and where they need to improve. If you withhold negative comments, the team members, not knowing that problem areas exist, will continue to make similar mistakes.

Rewards

If you want a team's exceptional performance to continue, recognize and reward it. This is a simple, fundamental rule of management, and one that many managers ignore. Such a failure can undermine both your and a team member's effectiveness, and can create major obstacles to accomplishing the goals of the department.

Wise managers reward exceptional performance with exceptional salary increases, promote individuals who consistently perform well, and frequently thank everyone whose efforts they appreciate.

Chapter 21

Negotiate to a Win

The skillful negotiator is the person who moves ahead in the business world. He or she has a skill that today is used in everything from getting a raise to delegating an unwanted assignment to reaching a manufacturing agreement worth billions.

In *Getting to Yes,* Roger Fisher and William Ury caution that negotiation is not a matter of making concessions or butting heads. They call for principled negotiations — deciding issues on their merits. When you bargain over positions, you get locked in and get sidetracked from meeting both parties' concerns. Agreement is less likely.

Four Negotiation Points

Principled negotiation has four basic points:

1. Separate the people from the problem, the relationship from the substance of the negotiation. Try to view the situation from the other person's perspective and provide opportunities for both of you to express your emotions. Pay attention, listen, and do whatever you can to build a working relationship.

2. Focus on interests, not positions. You know your interests, the ones that have caused you to take your position. Now try to figure out the other parties'. Acknowledge their interests; give the people on the other side positive support equal in strength to the vigor with which you emphasize the problem.

3. Invent options for mutual gain. Then broaden your options, looking for room to negotiate. Look for mutual gain by identifying shared interests. These opportunities exist in every negotiation. Stress them to make negotiations smoother and more amicable.

Make the other person's decision easy. Look for possible agreements early in the process.

4. Insist on objective criteria. That takes advance preparation and evaluation of alternatives.

Frame each issue as a joint search for objective criteria, as if you assume the other party is doing the same thing. Reason soundly and be open to reason. But yield only to principle, not pressure. When you feel pressure, invite the other side to state its reasoning. Then suggest objective criteria, and refuse to budge except on this basis.

Problem Negotiations

Sometimes, Fisher and Ury note, you're not negotiating on a level playing field. The other side may be richer, better connected, with a larger staff, or have more powerful weapons. You can't change that, but you can protect yourself from making a bad agreement. Before negotiations start, know the worst outcome you'll accept. Keep that in mind as your bottom line. At the same time, make the most of your assets. Know what you'll do if the negotiations fail. Be willing to break off negotiations if you can't reach an acceptable agreement.

You may encounter opponents who won't budge from their positions. Don't push back. Silence is your best weapon. It can create the impression of a stalemate, which the other side will be impelled to break by offering something different.

Do Your Homework

More advice is offered by David D. Seltz and Alfred J. Modica in *Negotiate Your Way to Success*.

Never lose sight of the fact that settlements are negotiated because they're beneficial to both sides. Before you enter the negotiation, do your homework, including these steps:

- **Research.** Amass factual information to back up the case you want to make.
- **Psychological detective work.** Think about your adversary. Likes? Dislikes? Flexible? Narrow-minded?
- **Self-evaluation.** What are your strengths and weaknesses?
- **Plan your strategy.** What will happen if you get what you want? When, where, and how will the negotiations be scheduled?
- **Practice.** Actually rehearse the negotiations, using another person as the devil's advocate.

Setting the Stage

Leave nothing to chance. One of the most basic details is the place and time of the negotiating session. A neutral location is preferable. A "home team" always has an advantage that makes the visitors resentful and is a detriment to a successful negotiation. Keep the meeting free of distractions. Best time? Most individuals are at their peak efficiency at about 11 a.m. Early in the week is better, too. Never negotiate on Friday. People are thinking about the weekend.

Commitment: the Vital Factor

Start by identifying the committed parties, the person or persons in position to sit down with you and negotiate. If one is obviously not right, broaden the discussion group to include others. And remember that commitment and negotiation are not inevitable. Sometimes the opportunity to negotiate is just not there.

Dressing Up the Negotiations

Use props and personal attitudes to dress up your negotiations and build credibility and impact. Start off with an air of formality. It gives you room to maneuver that you lose if you open more casually.

Use some sort of prop to help you to control the pace of the session. Carefully prepared research notes, blank legal pad and pen, videotape, or audio tape will help.

Hand your adversary something — a photocopy of your material, perhaps — that captures his attention and allows you to lead the conversation.

Consult a special prop, such as an expert or consultant in your field of endeavor.

Using Leverage

Leverage is the ability to get multiple benefits from your assets. Truthful self-evaluation is the key to the successful use of leverage.

If you have a certain character, admit it and use it to your own advantage. Glenn W. Turner, who built a quick empire with his "Dare to be Great" organization, started with a serious problem for a door-to-door salesman — a distinct and glaring harelip. He capitalized on it. "I see you're looking at my harelip, ma'am," he said to prospects. "Heck, it's just something I put on this morning so a pretty lady like you would notice me."

Use leverage to maximize your efforts. Don't waste it in unproductive gambits with your adversary. Many people negotiating for a job begin with two strikes against them because their résumé includes too much that is not applicable to the job. Be selective. Negotiation is communication. Don't confuse the main issues by heaping on irrelevant factors.

Never abuse your adversary. You'll get a lot more by using "I really wish I could afford to pay you what this fine old house is worth" than with "This old junk pile is about to fall over, and it will take a lot to get it in shape, so here's my top offer."

For every gain you make, give something back in return, even if it is little more than a formality.

It's important to you to have clearly in your mind what you want and what you can afford to give up. The shortest distance between two positions in negotiations is never a straight line.

Keep It Simple

The successful negotiator is an expert at clarifying and conveying a point of view to an adversary. Never be afraid of offending someone with simplicity.

First, break up your discussion into compact and understandable little bites of information and begin to chew on them with your adversary. Next, let your adversary swallow and digest. But don't take on faith that all key points have been communicated. Keep returning to them. A little redundancy won't hurt. Most individuals actually enjoy hearing information they have just learned.

You're Succeeding

There are five key signs that negotiations are turning in your direction:

1. Fewer counterarguments.

2. Both sides' points are closer together.

3. The other person talks about final arrangements.

4. The other person extends a personal invitation to you and your spouse.

5. The other person is willing to put the agreement in writing.

Cement the completed negotiations by meeting to sign. Never put the formal agreement in the mail.

Be a good winner. Don't gloat. You're in the game for the long run. Send the other person a thank-you letter, noting that you look forward to a long working relationship.

International Negotiations

Jack Nadel, who wrote *Cracking the Global Market,* is a veteran of years of negotiations, here and abroad. His advice on the subject is down-to-earth and practical, and it applies both to the international field and to the most simple of deals.

His thinking differs in marked fashion from the authors we just quoted. His first guideline is: "Get away from the other side of the desk." This means ridding yourself of an adversary role. The reality is that you have a mutual problem which you are going to solve to your mutual advantage. Your intention and the intention of the person with whom you are negotiating must be to structure a deal that resolves the problem and gives each of you what you want.

It's not always possible. When it can't be done, it's better to make no deal than to make a poor deal.

Much of your work must be done before you approach the negotiating table. You must learn all you can about what you want to accomplish, the product, the market, and the people with whom you will be negotiating.

Visualization

Visualization is a technique you can use that can spell the difference between success and failure. It means acting out in your mind the logical actions of what you are going to do — before you do it.

"I first complete all of my homework on the deal," Nadel says. "Then I turn on the screen in my mind. I see myself entering the room where we will negotiate. I see the people, and we introduce each other and start our conversation.

"I run the tape all the way through to the end — through the objections, the price levels, the counteroffers, the reactions, the banter, everything. I do the entire meeting in my mind."

Note that this isn't just thinking about the meeting. It's going through it in your mind. Then, when Nadel goes into the real meeting, it's as if he were entering it for the second time. He says that most of the time he is 60 to 70 percent right as to what happens. That gives him an enormous advantage.

It has had different results for him. Sometimes he's gone through the visualization, felt lousy about it, and passed on the deal.

Starting the Negotiations

Nadel has a formula for starting negotiations. Get the other person to answer this question: "Look, if you could write the script for the deal that you want, what would you want?" Sometimes that person will ask for less than what you are willing to pay.

Don't be greedy. That's trying to wring the last drop of blood out of someone in negotiation. It can blow deals, destroy relationships, and ruin businesses. It's totally unnecessary, too. If there's not enough fair profit in the deal for both, move to something else.

Chapter 22

Make Meetings Worthwhile

Meetings are a fact of business life, but most of them are frustrating and time-consuming. The results are rarely worth the time and effort of the many people involved.

Yet meetings are a sensible way to handle many kinds of discussions, problem-solving sessions, presentations, and general updates on what's happening.

If you learn to plan, structure, and participate in meetings effectively, you will be able to improve your own time management and productivity as well as that of other participants.

Room for Improvement

And there is a lot of room for improvement. In *We've Got to Start Meeting Like This,* authors Roger K. Mosvick and Robert B. Nelson reported on a poll of managers and professionals to identify the specific problems of meetings. These participants listed 1,305 problems. The top one was that meetings too often get off the subject. Others, in order of rank were, no goals or agendas, too lengthy, poor or inadequate preparation, inconclusive, disorganized, and ineffective leadership/lack of control.

Less than 10 percent of all meetings have agendas, says *Listen!* author Thomas E. Anastasi, Jr. But an agenda is essential if participants are to prepare for meetings by gathering relevant information.

Even better is a timed agenda that tells participants in advance that they will deal with topic A from 9 to 10, topic B from 10 to 11, and so on. That way, participants can attend only at the times when they can contribute and benefit.

Before the Meeting

If a meeting is to be effective, preparation must start long before the meeting leader greets the participants.

Determine the purpose of the meeting. But before you set the date, consider the other available communications media. If the most effective is a meeting, follow these guidelines. If not, forget the meeting and use another more effective medium.

Select the participants on the basis of their abilities to contribute to and profit from the meeting. If participation and discussion are important — and they are — limit the number of participants to five or six. It's difficult for a dozen or more people to participate effectively in a discussion.

Prepare a draft agenda. List the items the meeting can usefully discuss, and the times allotted to each topic. Circulate this draft agenda to the participants, and set a firm return date for comments.

Prepare the Firm Agenda

Having received the comments on the draft agenda, prepare the firm agenda. Include the topics to be discussed, the date, time, place of the meeting, a list of participants and their functions, and, to help manage the distracting interruptions for your meeting, an indication on how messages will be delivered to participants during breaks in the meeting.

Arrange the logistics. These include the room, any necessary audio-visual support that is needed, and the amenities such as ashtrays, pencils, notepaper, water, and glasses. Also arrange for coffee breaks and meals, if necessary.

If persons from out of town will participate, coordinate travel and hotel arrangements.

Prepare sufficient copies of any documents to be used at the meeting. If the flow of the meeting would be smoothed by an advance reading of such documents, send them to participants.

Name a Leader

Select a meeting leader on the basis of ability to make the meeting work. Select someone else to take notes, if this is necessary.

Prepare an attendance sheet, not to record truancy but to help the note-taker prepare the meeting minutes.

At the Last Minute

Just before the meeting, check on the documents you will hand out. Visit the site in advance to make certain it is ready. Set up and focus any audio-visual equipment.

Conducting the Meeting

Start on time. The people who are on time deserve this courtesy. It assures all participants that this will be an orderly meeting which deserves their listening attention.

If participants do not know each other, introduce them by name and function. Name badges may help. The badges can be prepared in advance, or the participants can write their own names if given blank cards and felt-tip markers.

Tell the participants where they can find rest rooms, a coffee machine, telephones, and whatever else they may need. This promotes listening, since participants won't be wondering about these things later when they should be listening.

Review the agenda. Reinforce the purpose of the meeting. Modify the agenda as needed to take care of any last-minute developments.

Summarize Action

As you move into consideration of the agenda items, summarize and note action items or agreements.

Keep your eye on the clock and match the meeting's pace with the time available. If people know that your meeting will start and end on time, they won't be distracted by worry that the meeting will run overtime.

End on time.

After the Meeting

Prepare the minutes promptly. Minutes are not a transcript. They should be concise, giving the meeting date, time, place, and purpose, the names of those who attended, any conclusions, agreements, action items, or assignments. They may also list open items.

The minutes should not try to summarize the discussion or point out who said what and who disagreed with whom.

Finally, review the meeting in your own mind. What did you learn that would be useful in planning, conducting, and following up other meetings?

The Planning Process

Roger K. Mosvick and Robert B. Nelson go even deeper into the meeting planning process.

They recommend writing down the purpose of the meeting in one clear sentence, the expected outcomes in another. For example: "To decide on a marketing plan and determine implementation responsibilities for everyone in the group. To be completed by July."

Meeting Formats

Meetings usually have one of these formats:

● **Consultation.** This is for an ad hoc group, usually called on short notice and for a specific decision. Supervisors call them to get input on a problem. The supervisor should listen as much as possible. Participant input is spontaneous, usually without the benefit of long consideration. The supervisor chairs the meeting and clearly is responsible for the final decision.

● **Recommendation.** This meeting is more formal, lasts longer, and features independent deliberations by the group. The manager meets with the group to outline the problem, then leaves the group to conduct deliberations. It is clear that while the group will choose its own leadership and decision process, the manager retains final decision power, and can reject all recommendations.

This meeting is particularly valuable in companies where convening supervisors come and go, so committee members take their assignments seriously.

● **Delegation.** The manager delegates complete decision-making responsibility to a group of trusted subordinates. Such meetings are less frequent because managers fear they will lose control. There is no more powerful demonstration of trust and respect than the delegated decision. Once this course is taken, the manager must let the group work out the solution without intervention or later modification. One of the worst errors a manager can make is to delegate a decision, then intervene in the decision process.

No matter which format is selected, the manager should report back to the committee on the final decision.

Planning Checklist

Here is a checklist prepared by Mosvick and Nelson to help meeting planners:

_____ Write the purpose and general objectives of the meeting.
_____ Select the type of format and leadership style.
_____ Decide who will attend.
_____ Select a chairperson.
_____ Decide how and when participants will be notified of their tasks.
_____ Pick the time, place, and duration of the meeting.
_____ Compose an agenda.
_____ Name a recorder to report on results.
_____ Decide who will have responsibility for implementation steps and action items.

Leading a Meeting

The successful meeting leader or chairperson is the person who can adapt leadership styles to different groups, different members, and different tasks. The failure is the person who uses one role, usually authoritarian, when the group expects another.

Much of the role of the leader is linked with the purpose of a meeting. Meeting to inform subordinates of a decision calls for one approach; a completely different one is needed if the meeting is to gain their commitment to carry out a decision made by others.

Decision-Making

Managers call most meetings to gather informed opinions from expert subordinates or colleagues to help make decisions for which the manager is responsible. Managers need to tap the expertise of their subordinates and to use them as sounding boards for the managers' ideas.

In this situation, managers who overemphasize their own contributions do more harm than good by inhibiting the contributions of the others.

Leaders should consider participants as equals, each to be respected for having information and judgment at least equal to and often superior to the leader's. This attitude sets an appropriate tone for the meeting.

A strong leader often errs by not being willing to share chairperson functions and by reacting sharply to perceived dominance by group participants. This style may be appropriate when meeting procedures and mechanics are discussed, so the chairperson can monitor and direct progress, but if used in other areas, it will discourage creative contributions.

Dissent is Essential

Effective leaders recognize that dissent is essential. The purpose of many meetings is to scrutinize ideas in order to reach the best decision possible. The alternative is the agreement of "yes-men" who withhold negative information.

Group leaders need to make it plain that disagreement and constructive criticism are encouraged and expected in group deliberations. It is the only way to achieve free and open participation in decision-making. One of the best techniques used by chairpersons to accomplish this is to refuse to take sides in a dispute until all evidence is presented.

Leaders must make absolutely clear the roles of participants in decision-making. This means spelling out whether any committee conclusion is a recommendation or a decision. To do otherwise invites bad feelings and plummeting morale.

Managers jealous of their rank have been known to shift goals in the middle of a committee's work, or to fail to give any feedback to a group about its recommendations. Such practices are fundamentally bad management.

Orientation Speech

The chairman should kick off the meeting with an orientation speech lasting from three to five minutes. This should serve as the foundation of the entire decision process. It also orients the group on the meeting's purpose and procedures, provides an information base, and reaches clear agreement on how the group can proceed.

A good orientation speech can cut meeting time in half and increase the probability of a better decision.

Checklist for Speech

Here's a checklist to use when preparing your orientation speech:

- State the problem, general objectives, ,and procedures.
- Provide the information base, including present status and consequences if not resolved.
- Define the territory, the topics you'll discuss and the boundaries of the discussion. Set criteria for a good solution.
- Review the agenda, then ask for any changes.
- Appoint a recorder, (who knows of this in advance) and explain the recorder's role.

While it takes time to prepare this speech, it doesn't take half as long as a meeting that gets off track.

Chairman's Responsibilities

As chairman, you have certain responsibilities during the meeting. By carrying them out, you'll do much to insure the success of the meeting.

- Start on time.
- Build a permissive climate.
- Follow the agenda.
- Give or get accurate summaries.
- Give or get clarification of vague statements.
- Encourage evaluation of all generalizations.
- Protect the expression of minority opinions.
- Minimize conflict over issues that have nothing to do with the meeting.
- Try to reach a consensus on all conclusions.
- End the meeting by reviewing accomplishments, answering questions, and specifying actions to be taken, and by whom.
- End the meeting on time.

The Participant's Role

Your role as a meeting participant isn't a passive one. You should prepare for the meeting, and then have something to offer. You should be prepared to influence the group effectively and manage conflict if it arises.

If you have been told about a meeting, but haven't received an agenda, ask the chairperson for one.

Conduct research into problems that will be discussed so that you can offer stimulating, well-grounded views. If you're strongly involved in the problem, try to sell in advance your ideas to other group members.

There is much that you and other participants can do to make a meeting more successful.

First, organize your contributions. Think before you speak. If what you will say is complicated, rehearse it before the meeting. Make one point at a time. Speak clearly and forcefully, offering valid evidence rather than vague statements.

Listen to the discussion. Then speak when your contribution is relevant. If the conversation has moved past your point, don't try to backtrack. And when you are listening, monitor your non-verbal signals. Facial expressions can speak volumes. So can yawns and doodling.

How to Influence Groups

If you want to influence your group's deliberations, try to speak in the first five minutes of discussion of a topic. Speak frequently. Talk each time for thirty seconds or so. But don't feel obligated to respond to every point mentioned. Limit yourself to good ideas. Speak fast, fluently, and forcefully. (Rehearsing what you'll say helps here.)

State your idea, relate its significance, support it with evidence, then ask for responses.

Those Worthless Sessions

Ever the realist, Charles R. Hobbs recognizes that on occasion you will be roped into attending a meeting that promises little and produces less.

What to do?

- Ask if there are any further contributions you can make. If not, leave.
- Have your secretary or someone else call for you with "urgent" business elsewhere.
- Use meeting time to plan or write.
- Put your mind on something more productive.
- Sit in the back of the room and slip out when the meeting is no longer productive for you.
- Tell your boss that you feel you could be more productive if you didn't lose so much time in unproductive meetings.

Chapter 23

Leadership: The Real Test

If you're ambitious, you probably envision yourself becoming a leader, an individual who others respect and follow.

Leadership is not limited to the person at the top of the pyramid. It's a mix of traits and skills that you can develop at any time and that will help move you up the ladder.

Harold Geneen, a recognized business leader, gives his version of what it takes in *Managing*.

Management and leadership are intertwined, Geneen says.

Business management is something objective. You want to get from here to there, and your performance can be measured. What's more, you can be taught the tools of the trade in a school of business administration.

Leadership is something else again.

It is purely subjective, virtually impossible to measure objectively, and can't be taught in school.

Leadership is the ability to inspire other people to work together as a team, following your lead, in order to attain a common objective. The ability to lead is acquired through the experience of everyday life.

Getting People to Follow

Leaders try to get people to reach for goals they may think are beyond them. They try to get people to accomplish more than they think is possible.

They do this by running the kind of work place where it is possible for workers to enjoy the process of tackling a difficult job and solving it. They make people realize that in working this way, they are part of a team, and each one is a valued contributor to that team.

Show Appreciation

In that connection, leaders let team members know that they are needed and appreciated, so they can take pride and satisfaction from playing a winning game.

Leaders create a climate of growth and opportunity, a climate in which all want to carry their fair share and to excel. The leaders do this in part by unlocking any inhibitions or fears that may contribute to making people insecure.

The mark of a leader is a willingness to provide participatory leadership. That means being willing to grab an oar and pull with other team members. Leaders set an example for others by working long hours, not merely telling others to do this.

Finally, says Geneen, they're not satisfied with mediocre results. If they were, that's exactly what they would get.

Leadership Styles

In *The Creative Edge,* William C. Miller describes five leadership styles in common use.

1. **Tell.** "Based on my decision, here's what I want you to do."
2. **Sell.** "Based on my decision, here's what I want you to do because . . ."
3. **Consult.** "Before I make a decision, I want your input."
4. **Participate.** "We need to make a decision together."
5. **Delegate.** "You make a decision."

Delegation can be made at three levels:

1. **Ask:** "Produce this result, and ask me before you take any action."
2. **Inform.** "Produce this result, and keep me informed of what action you have taken."
3. **Do.** "Produce this result, and I don't need to know what you have done."

Miller notes that participation is widely promoted today, but it is not always desirable.

Would you want a participatory style of leadership if you were a passenger in a nose-diving airplane?

A Leader's Abilities

The authors of *Back-to-Basics Management* say a leader has the power to shape and mold an organization through group cooperation. This calls for many abilities. Among them:

- Recognize weaknesses and strengths in yourself and others.
- Set goals and meet them.
- Pass on credit to others for personal contributions.
- Find and use the right resource to accomplish a task.
- Measure the degree of success or failure in an operation.
- Turn every situation into a learning experience.
- Understand the use of power. Accept it in your position.
- Deal with the present realistically, while retaining the stuff of which dreams are made.
- Constantly strive to know and understand more about everything.

- Discriminate between truth, wishful thinking, and hard facts.
- Awaken those around you to an understanding of their full potential.

Skills of Leadership

Get to know the tangible and intangible needs of everyone in your group. Give them what satisfies their needs. Each time you reinforce this capability of yours, they will become more loyal, more cohesive, more motivated.

You should concentrate on certain basic actions.

One of these is to process information, not just job information, and use it. Form premises that lead to useful conclusions. Be innovative, able to take the information and resources at hand and give your people the competitive edge.

Finally, continue gathering the knowledge and honing the skills that complement your position as a leader.

Setting an Example

John Adair, who wrote *Effective Leadership,* emphasizes that one of the most important moves a leader can make is to set an example.

He makes a good point: You set an example whether you want to or not. The trick is to set a good example, to be what you want others to be.

Example is important because people take in information more through their eyes than through their ears. What they see you do has far greater impact than what they hear you say. Word and example must match up, must not conflict.

If bosses set office hours from nine to five, but show up at ten and leave at four, if the mistakes of others are fodder for public discussion, but theirs are never mentioned, expect that behavior to become contagious. Then subordinates will realize it's impossible to follow the leader's example without getting into trouble, and they will become frustrated.

Francis Bacon said it well: "He that gives good advice builds with one hand. He that gives good counsel and example builds with both. But he that gives good admonition and bad example builds with one hand and pulls down with the other."

A good leader uses creative power, especially if it involves an element of self-sacrifice. Seeing this can work in people's minds to alter their ways. The process may take time, but the leader whose example backs up his words puts himself in an unassailable position. No one can accuse him of hypocrisy.

"Leadership is example," wrote one officer cadet at military school, making that perhaps the shortest and at the same time the most vivid definition of leadership.

Pitfalls of Success

A leader is ultimately the person at the top of the pyramid, the person who has made it.

But there's no more security at the top than anywhere else. As Raymond C. Johnson points out in *The Achievers,* success sets traps for the unwary that keep you from achieving your full potential.

One of the most difficult problems to conquer when you reach the top is the ivory tower syndrome, or executive isolation. The farther an executive moves from the roots of the business, the harder it is to keep up with what's happening in that business.

Avoid Isolation

Most executives work and live and lunch and play golf or tennis with the same people. That means that all of their person-to-person contact is with people who live, work, and think alike.

This gradual isolation from reality is a trap you must fight from the beginning of your rise in the organization. You must work to keep lines of communication open, and you must make certain that communication comes up to you from the bottom.

There are many tried and true methods to achieve this. You can use advisory committees, market and employee surveys, and suggestion boxes. One of your musts should be maintaining contact with customers. Another is to make sure you are getting good information from a wide variety of sources.

A leader has the responsibility and authority for making the final decision. He may not always get credit when things go right, but he'll get the blame when things go wrong. So it's critical to have a total grasp of the situation before making decisions.

Take It in Stride

Another common pitfall of success is getting carried away with the excellence of one's own work. Once you start believing your own press releases, you're in trouble.

A successful achiever can be overwhelmed with excessive praise to the point that he stops forward progress.

The key is to learn to take it all in stride — the successes and the failures. Both are usually temporary, and both provide valuable lessons.

When you think you have the whole world in the palm of your hand and that there's no one quite like you, stop. Don't think of the great things you've done. Instead, think of all the things that still need to be done.

Then get started.